Advice From The Blender

*What to know before you blend
so nobody gets creamed*

Susan J. Hetrick

xulon
PRESS

Copyright © 2007 by Susan J. Hetrick

Advice From The Blender
by Susan J. Hetrick

Printed in the United States of America

ISBN 978-1-60266-569-9

Author photograph by Arizona Eaton.
Cover design by Denise Nolf.
Edited by Andrea and Brian Garrett.

All rights reserved solely by the author. The author guarantees all contents are original and do not infringe upon the legal rights of any other person or work. No part of this book may be reproduced in any form without the permission of the author. The views expressed in this book are not necessarily those of the publisher.

Unless otherwise indicated, Bible quotations are taken from the NEW AMERICAN STANDARD BIBLE®. Copyright © 1960, 1962, 1963, 1968, 1971, 1972, 1973, 1975, 1977, 1995 by The Lockman Foundation. Used by permission.

www.xulonpress.com

What people are saying about *Advice From The Blender*

"An encouraging blend of real stepfamily stories and practical advice, Susan's book offers help and hope."

~ Ron L. Deal
Author of *The Smart Stepfamily* and
President, Successful Stepfamilies.com

"*Advice From the Blender* is an incredibly rich resource for those entering the world of blended families. Susan Hetrick uses numerous examples from an expansive cross-section of people. She does a phenomenal job of addressing the challenges that the couples face in bringing together two families, as well as issues the children may struggle to overcome. The questions at the end of each chapter are a must-do; they will encourage honest communication and revelation. For those that are on the brink of blending or those who are established as a blended family, this book will give you a renewed sense of hope and purpose."

~ Eric and Jennifer Garcia
Co-Founders, Association of Marriage and Family Ministries (AMFM)

"*Advice from the Blender* is a wonderful book, filled with practical suggestions every stepfamily can use. You'll meet real-life stepfamilies who candidly share their trials and triumphs, and learn some valuable lessons about stepfamily success."

~ Jeff and Judi Parziale
Co-Directors, InStep Ministries

"With timeless wisdom and sly humor, Susan Hetrick offers blended families wisdom gained from her own experience. Whether you are considering the step of blending families or are currently caught-up in that challenging whirl, this book is a *must-read*."

~ Sandra D. Wilson, Ph.D.
Retired family therapist and
Author of *Released From Shame* and
Shame-Free Parenting

Contents

Acknowledgements ix

Introduction xi

The Families – Living in the Blender xv

Chapter 1 19
    And we'll live happily ever after… – Stepfamily expectations and roles

Chapter 2 33
    We both have baggage…but it's cute and it matches – Dealing with the past, and making your marriage your #1 priority

Chapter 3 53
    The Package Deal – Bonding as a family without resorting to Superglue or duct tape

Chapter 4 69
    The Infiltrator…and other names for stepparents – Helping the kids adjust

Chapter 5 87
    Choosing your battles – Blending parenting skills

Chapter 6 105
    In-laws, Outlaws and Theories of Relativity – The "ex-tended" family experience

Chapter 7 119
    Holidays and other worst-case scenarios – What blending *really* means

Chapter 8 131
    The House Blend – Your family blending recipe

Appendix A: 143
    Resources for blended families

Appendix B: 151
    Bible verses for blended families

Notes 159

In Appreciation

⊚

My most sincere and heart-felt thanks go to:

Diane Larson-Lippard: for the priceless idea of a book-writing internship, for all of your prayers and our many lunches;

Dr. Sandra Wilson: for your encouragement, wisdom and great advice;

Amy Brandais: for proofreading the first chapters, your helpful suggestions and for putting up with *all* of us staying in your house – twice;

Brian and Andrea Garrett: for your editorial expertise;

Denise Nolf: for the fabulous cover;

Maria, Maruja, y Tío Alfredo: *por demostrarme el significado de la familia*;

The Families who worked with me on this project (you know who you are): for honestly answering all my silly questions,

Advice From The Blender

telling me your stories, and for sticking with your families no matter what;

The members of the Association of Marriage and Family Ministries (AMFM): for your prayers, encouragement and support;

The faculty, staff and students of Phoenix Seminary: for the blessing of your friendship, for cheering me on, and your Godly wisdom that helped me proceed;

John & Nancy Peck and Dave & Carolyn Hetrick: for being great parents, grandparents, and terrific examples of strong marriages, and for nagging me to finish this book (Carolyn!);

Arizona, Montana, Lysa and Chase: for your awesome suggestions and great hugs, for forcing me to watch funny movies and listen to loud music, and for letting me drive you all over town – I love you all more than I could ever put into words, "ooxxOXooXXx";

My soul mate David: for all your love, confidence, and great advice; for making me take long walks with you and the dogs, and for the endless pots of coffee – I love you with all my heart;

And to my God – Father, Savior, Spirit: for the calling and gifts you have blessed me with, for the tropical fish dreams, for loving me and for everything else.

Introduction

Many stepfamily advocates have a problem with the term *blended family*. They claim that no family really blends without someone getting creamed. I respectfully disagree. Others have problems with the term "step" in reference to stepparents, and use terms like *co-parents*, which just sounds odd. I have also heard the terms *Bonus-Mom* and *Bonus-Dad*, which are interesting, but then we run into their counterparts: *Bio-Mom* and *Bio-Dad*, which just sound like poorly-drawn cartoon superheroes and sets up a joke about *Biohazards*. Everyone seems to have their individual preferences about what a stepfamily and its various members should be called. However, far more important than what we call blended families is how they relate to one another as they move into the blender and their story begins.

My husband David and I have been married since 2004. We have been best friends since junior high school. We never dated each other during high school – we were just friends. We went to different colleges, separated by 2,000 miles, but kept in touch with letters and phone calls. He and his first wife came to my first wedding, and we exchanged Christmas cards and pictures of our children through the years. We went through divorces around the same time, and commiserated via e-mail.

Advice From The Blender

In 2002, David invited me to accompany him "on a work thing" which turned out to be a seven-day Caribbean cruise. He understandably didn't want to take his ex-wife, and thought I might enjoy a vacation since I had been a working, single mother for almost a year. I agreed to go, but only with the understanding that we were going *just as friends* – nothing more.

On the cruise David's assistant kept introducing me to people as "David's date" to which I insisted, "It's not a date!" Alas, who knew a Caribbean cruise would be romantic? By the third day I decided that this was the best date I'd ever been on.

All told, we had seven dates over a year and a half. They all began in an airport, since David lived in Michigan and I lived in Nevada. We each have a daughter and a son from our previous marriages, and we dated long-distance for almost a full year before we introduced the children to each other. It was a match made in heaven: my kids liked him, his kids liked me, and they all liked each other. We *thought* we were doing everything right.

When we began to think about getting married and blending our families we heard it all: "You're perfect for each other! What took you so long?" and "Just like the *Brady Bunch*!" and my personal favorite, "Since you have kids, you should wait at least five years after your divorce before you even begin dating." (Too late. And really – *five years*?!)

We read what books we could find by the "experts" – which were few – and listened to advice from our friends and families about communication, finances and all of the other things that one discusses before getting married. However, no one seemed to know what to tell us about blending two adults, four children, two dogs, one cat and a hamster into one semicohesive family. We had lots of information about marriage, but not much about stepfamilies.

Advice From The Blender

Apparently, we weren't the only ones. According to Barna Research, about 43% of all marriages in the United States are remarriages for at least one of the adults, and more than 65% of those remarriages involve children from previous relationships, forming stepfamilies. However, 65 to 70% of all remarriages involving children eventually end in divorce[1]. That is a horrifying statistic, but one that is understandable, since the only easily accessible information about blending families comes from reruns of *The Brady Bunch*!

There are several excellent stepfamily resources out there, but they are not heavily advertised or always on the front rack at your local bookstore. And strangely enough, hunting down resources that deal with blended family issues when you don't even envision yourselves *having* issues isn't a top priority when you're in love, planning a wedding, moving into a new home, and dealing with the children's schedules all at the same time!

Granted, premarital counseling is now available through most churches and many counseling offices. Some of these programs focus on the unique challenges facing remarriages. However, using this type of counseling as a preemptive resource *for the entire family* has not been widely done. Also, there are families for which counseling is impractical, financially or geographically prohibitive, or simply not feasible.

This book is an attempt to remedy those situations. It was born from our own blending experience, and sound advice compiled from the experiences of real stepfamilies from all over the United States. These families were generous enough to share "the good, the bad and the ugly" about blending; what to look forward to, what to watch out for, what challenges they faced and most importantly what has worked for them. Some of the names and specific identifying information about the families involved have been changed out of respect for their privacy.

It is my intent that this book will help stepcouples and their children navigate the rough road toward blending more easily. There are certain chapters that focus only on the stepcouple, others that focus on the children, and several chapters that focus on the anticipated stepfamily as a whole. Working through the book *together as a family* will assist everyone involved to become aware of some of the emotional roadblocks that are common in stepfamilies and explore everyone's feelings about the upcoming marriage. *This is especially important for the children involved.* However, all of the advice in this book is equally applicable to families that have been in stepfamily mode for a while, so even if you're already married and 'living in the blender', it's never too late to mend any damage or renovate the structure of your family.

The main reason for writing this book is that David and I really could have used this advice when we got married. And so, for those about to move into the blender, this book is a collection of stories and advice from some of us who already live there. Welcome to the blender!

The Families: Living in the Blender

Both Tony (35) and Angela (33) were widowed prior to their marriage two years ago. Combined, they have five children living with them in a suburb of Boston: his 4-year-old twin boys, her 3-year-old twin girls, and their 6-month-old son. Tony works in construction, and Angela stays at home with the children.

Sloane (40), an artist, and Jason (43), a catering chef, have been married for three years and live in Mesa, Arizona. They each have a daughter and a son, all of whom live with them. Jason's former wife lives five miles away and has a flexible visitation schedule with Cassidy (10) and Cole (8). Sloane's former husband has remarried and lives in another state. He sees their children Alisha (14) and Thatcher (12), during Christmas and summer vacations.

Barry (47), an attorney, has been married to a professional actress, Jennifer (46), for nine years. They live in New York City. This is the second marriage for both of them. She has two children, Sasha (17) and Alexa (15). Barry has no biological children.

Advice From The Blender

Karl (87) and Marjorie (86) are retired and live in Bradenton, Florida. They have been married for two years. This is the second marriage for both of them and collectively they have seven children, 18 grandchildren, 22 great-grandchildren!

Lori (41), a stay-at-home mom, and Matt (51), an attorney, have been married for six years and live in San Diego, California. She has two children by her first marriage, a boy Taylor (16) and a girl Darcy (14). Matt had previously been married three times and has no biological children.

Kelly (35) and Randy (45) have been married for two years. They live in Charleston, South Carolina and are both employed by a large Christian church. Randy's first marriage lasted 13 years, and he has full custody of his two daughters, Brooke (15) and Amber (12). This is Kelly's first marriage. She had two previous live-in relationships, and no biological children.

Sheila (34), a teacher, and Tim Smith (36), a school principal, have been married for one year. Sheila has two sons from a previous marriage, Derek (15) and Kyle (13). Tim is the father of their son Nicky (3), and daughter Jillian (6 months). They met at their church in Santa Fe, New Mexico and lived together for four years before marrying. Sheila grew up in an alcoholic and abusive home.

Rob (45), a former NFL player and president of a large corporation, and Kendra (41), an accountant, live in a suburb of Seattle. They have been married for five years and both have two teenagers. Kendra's girls are Leah (17) and Kara (16) and Rob's children are Kristy (16) and Eric (15).

Advice From The Blender

Karen (38), a bank manager, and Jon (33), a police officer, have been married for seven years. They live in central Texas. Karen shares custody of her daughter Mandy (13) with her ex-husband, and Jon shares custody of his daughter, Ariel (9) with his ex-wife. Five years ago Karen and Jon had a son, Dylan. Their family expanded again last fall with the sudden death of Jon's brother. Jon and Karen became the legal guardians for Jon's teenage nephews, Steven (16) and Daniel (14).

Monica (25), a stay-at-home mom and Steve (37), a Casino executive from Las Vegas, Nevada, were married a little more than a year ago. Monica's son, Cameron (5), lives with them full-time and sees his father on weekends. Steve's two daughters, Lindy (8) and Hailey (10), divide their time equally between their mother and father, alternating homes every other week.

Terri (34), a stay-at-home mom, and John (40), a pastor, of Boulder, Colorado had both been divorced for several years before meeting one another at church. Terri's daughter Amanda (5) and son Andrew (7) seemed to enjoy having a big brother, Jake (10) and a stepfather.

Brit (46), a retired Marine, and Melanie (36), a teacher, live in Atlanta, Georgia. Brit has two sons by his first marriage: Javon (22) and Jamal (21), both of whom are in the Air Force. Brit's second wife died shortly after the birth of their daughter, Jasmine (5). Melanie was previously married and has no biological children, but legally adopted Jasmine shortly after their wedding in 2003.

Doreen, a realtor, and Bill, a surgeon, live in Phoenix, Arizona. They are in their 50s and have been married for 12 years. As a career woman with no children of her own, becoming a stepmother to Bill's three grown children was a challenge for Doreen, and to become an instant stepgrandmother was a real eye-opener!

Elise (42), a human resources manager, and Scott (45), a mechanic, live in rural Montana on a ranch. They have been married nine years and have a son, Trey (6). It is Elise's first marriage, Scott's second. He has two daughters by his first marriage: Lark (18) and Katy (15). They rarely see his daughters.

CHAPTER 1

And we'll live happily ever after...
Stepfamily expectations and roles

*"Reality is merely an illusion –
albeit, a very persistent one".*
~ Albert Einstein

Everyone has expectations about life. We each view the world through our own unique lenses, and expect things to go a certain way. This is normal and understandable. The problems arise when our expectations and reality are not even in the same universe. After talking with stepfamilies around the country, it still amazes me that grown adults can have some of the most childlike expectations when it comes to their stepfamilies. (And then there are the kids' expectations!) Some of the commonly held unrealistic expectations that stepfamilies have include:

- The kids are just as excited about the wedding as we are.

- I know he/she has kids, but they won't affect *our* relationship.
- Everyone will get along and love one another ... instantly.
- I will love his/her children just like I do my own.
- We'll be just like *The Brady Bunch*; it'll be fun!
- Our parents will accept the stepkids without hesitation.
- What are one or two more kids?
- His/her ex-spouse is *history* and won't be involved in anything we do.
- And my all-time favorite: Change!? Why would anything change?

Reality Check

Don't feel bad if you hold some of these beliefs. We all have held on to unrealistic ideas at some point in our lives. However, if these expectations are unrealistic – and they are – what *should* you expect as you become a stepfamily? That is a valid question, but one that is extremely difficult to answer since stepfamilies are different from nuclear families and each stepfamily is unique.

Going Nuclear

Let's take a look at some of these differences. In a first-time nuclear family, where neither the husband nor the wife has been previously married, their life equation is:

1 woman + 1 man = 1 married couple

Their relationship is all about them. Ideally, they become engaged, have a wedding, go on a honeymoon, move in to their new home, and begin their life together. They work through whatever they need to work through and they grow together. The couple then may have a child. They work through whatever they need to work through, and they all grow together. Subsequently their life equation looks like this:

$$1 \text{ woman} + 1 \text{ man} + 1 \text{ child} = 1 \text{ family}$$

The family may expand through the birth of another child, they work through what they need to work through and they all grow together, and so on. To some extent their life occurs in *predictable* stages, and they are committed to each other as a family.

Anti-Nuclear Alliances

In a stepfamily, the couple may have one of eight (or more) possible marital combinations: the man may have been divorced and the woman may have been single; the woman may have been widowed and the man may have been single; they could have both been divorced or they could have both been widowed or one of each; one or both of them may have several divorces behind them; one or both of them may have children, and so on. Their life equation becomes extremely complex:

$$\begin{array}{c} 1 \text{ woman } (+/- 1^{st} \text{ husband}) + 2 \text{ children} \\ + 1 \text{ man } (+/- 1^{st} \text{ wife}) + 1 \text{ child } (+/- 2^{nd} \text{ wife}) + 1 \text{ child} \\ = 1 \text{ very complicated stepfamily} \end{array}$$

According to research done by Life Innovations in Minneapolis, Minnesota, the average American stepfamily has *40 members*. These include the stepcouple themselves, his children, her children and the children they may have together, their former spouses (and *their* new spouses, and *their* children), their siblings, their parents, their in-laws and let's not forget the former in-laws! The family tree quickly becomes a family forest[2].

Essentially, the stepcouple's relationship is not just about the couple – it is about many relationships *in addition* to the couple. Therefore, stepcouples must not expect their marriage to be like a first marriage – it *will* be different and there is nothing *wrong* with that.

****

Sloane (40), an artist, and Jason (43), a catering chef, have been married for three years and live in Mesa, Arizona. They each have a daughter and a son, all of whom live with them. Jason's former wife lives five miles away and has a flexible visitation schedule with Cassidy (10) and Cole (8). Sloane's former husband has remarried and lives in another state. He sees their children Alisha (14) and Thatcher (12) during Christmas and summer vacations.

Jason: *I guess I figured that not a lot would change when Sloane and I got married, other than we were moving into a new house together. We had dated for two years, our kids all got along fine, and our ex's seemed OK with the wedding. We were completely unprepared for the fallout!*

Sloane*: It was an absolute shock when Jason's ex-wife was suddenly at our new house like, everyday, going through the kids' clothes, making snide comments about clutter, and even complaining about what kind of food we bought! She opened up the fridge one day and, completely ignoring me, looked at Jason and said "Why didn't you buy organic milk? You know the kids can't tolerate this kind! And you bought the wrong kind of apples – they only eat the red ones, not these sour green things!" I was dumbfounded! I mean, first of all, this was my house, and she was acting like I wasn't* *even in the room. And second, I had successfully raised my two kids without ever spending $6.00 a gallon on organic milk.*

Jason*: It hadn't occurred to me or to any of us that my ex-wife would just walk in and rummage through our stuff. I guess I just thought she'd live her life, and I'd live my life. After the refrigerator episode I realized that I had to set up some boundaries with my ex.*

Sloane*: That was the least of our problems that first year believe it or not. When we moved, suddenly none of the kids could stand each other anymore, they were all mad at us for not asking their permission to get married, we had to deal with the girls screaming at each other over closet space, and the boys fighting over who got the top bunk ... it was complete chaos.*

****

Stepfamilies, by definition, include children. A stepfamily is: Any marriage in which at least one of the spouses becomes a stepparent *regardless of the age of the children.* When you marry a person with children you "marry" the children as well[3]. They are part of the package. Because of this, expect to be involved in the children's lives and expect them to be involved in yours to some extent.

****

Barry (47), an attorney, has been married to a professional actress Jennifer (46) for nine years. They live in New York City. This is the second marriage for both of them. She has two children, Sasha (17) and Alexa (15). Barry has no biological children.

Barry: *My fanciful illusions about becoming a stepfather and raising young (now teenaged) children did not, in any respect, turn out how I had envisioned. Sasha was not a warm, cuddly child that welcomed me with loving open arms and looked upon me with wonder or awe. He was aloof and emotionally distant even at a young age and seemed to view adults with suspicion. He was a constant challenge at school and at home, so there has never been much tranquility in our household. Alexa was a little more loving and more emotionally available.*

My parents had a very successful marriage and I attempted to replicate their parenting model in my new family. It's based on mutual love and respect, effusive displays of affection, finding joy in life, a very high work ethic and a drive to improve oneself. This model and my expectations needed to be drastically modified with my new family. Jen's son and daughter are both intelligent but see no point in excelling academically; they don't understand my work ethic. My standards of success are not their standards of success. Nevertheless, I have tried my best to become a good father to them. The lessons I have learned from the past nine years have been patience, patience and more patience! I've learned to accept our children for who they are and to enjoy their accomplishments and experiences and not filter or supplant them with what I would want.

Even though being a stepfather has been extremely challenging and did not really meet my expectations, I have never contemplated giving up, nor have I ever complained that this is not what I signed up for. That is not what a family is about. You cannot give up on your family or the ones you love. No one ever promised me that I would have a perfect family or that our kids would be trouble-free.

****

Chances are the children did not ask for your remarriage, nor did they want to become part of a stepfamily. Therefore, expect some degree of anger and rebellion over this issue no matter what age your children are. According to Drs. Jeff and Judi Parziale of InStep Ministries in Tucson, Arizona, "This is the emotional state that most children are in when their mom or dad decides to remarry: few are through the grieving process, most are just beginning to adjust to the new single parent household and settling in to the "routine" of shuttling between two parents. So, how does a parent determine if their child is "ready" for the remarriage? Examine the following indicators. If your child or children exhibit any of these, they are NOT ready:

- They are acting out at school or at home.
- New behaviors have emerged: bedwetting, hoarding food, immaturity.
- Eating or sleeping patterns have changed.
- Emotional swings, shyness, withdrawal.
- Child feels responsible for the divorce.
- Child vocally opposes the new marriage.[4]

In general, the younger the children are the easier a remarriage will be on them. This is by no means a hard and fast rule. While the reaction to the new marriage will look different in every stepfamily, sometimes it isn't pretty.

****

Karl (87) and Marjorie (86) are retired and live in Bradenton, Florida. They have been married for two years. This is the second marriage for both of them and collectively they have seven children, 18 grandchildren, 22 great-grandchildren!

Karl: *Marjorie and I have known each other for more than 60 years. Her husband Harry was my best friend and I was the best man in their wedding. We lived in the same town in Vermont. Our kids grew up together and we sometimes took vacations together like a big family. When my wife Betty died 20 years ago, Margie and Harry were there for me. I took care of Margie when Harry got Alzheimer's. We'd go to visit him together in the nursing home and then go out to lunch. When he passed away, marriage just seemed like a natural next step for us. Neither of us wanted to be alone and we certainly weren't going to shack up together, so we got married. We just couldn't believe the rubbish that her son dished out!*

Marjorie: *You'd think that our children would want us to be happy, but my son Ethan refused to come to our wedding, and he hasn't spoken to us since. For pity's sake! A grown man and he's acting like a spoiled little boy. It has been very hurtful. We may be old, but we're not dead! Why shouldn't we be happy?*

****

The best advice we can offer about forming stepfamilies is to give it time. Blending is not an event, it is a process. Processes take time. David and I married in February and my children, Zonie and Tanner, were living with us from the beginning. David's children, Lysa and Chase, were still living in Michigan with their mom until they all moved to Scottsdale in July. We had six months with just my two, and six weeks with just his two, while my kids were visiting their father. By the time school began in late August, we had all four kids together full-time and we watched them each warm up to the stepfamily one by one.

After the initial six to twelve-month warming up period each of our children "thawed out" in terms of their feelings about being in a stepfamily. They all seemed to have come to some sort of resolution – or resignation – that the stepparent and stepsiblings were here to stay. It was an interesting process to watch and we were encouraged to hear the kids refer to one another as sisters and brothers. None of them ever used the term "step" – and neither did we.

Yet, there are still times when it seems as if our family will never blend. Recently Lysa commented, "We're weird. Sometimes we go for days when everyone gets along, and we're nice to each other and as a family we're good. Then we have a day where we suck." In truth, I suppose this is true for all families, whether they are nuclear or step.

Most families we spoke with told us that as a new stepparent you should allow *at least* one full year – sometimes several full years – for each stepchild to acknowledge and accept that you are part of the household and that there is a new dynamic in the family. During that time do not expect them to love you or even to like you. Don't try to become their "new parent". Simply be a friend to your stepchild and don't expect anything from them. You might be lucky enough to get a "hello" once in a while but don't *expect* more.

Role Models

When you move into the blender, the dynamics of the entire family should be renegotiated. This includes not just the parenting and stepparenting roles but also the roles of husband, wife, children and siblings.

When we speak of marriage or family roles many people automatically assume we're talking about the "traditional" family: Dad goes to work, Mom stays home with kids and bakes cookies – the style of family life that was glorified in *Ozzie and Harriet*. While those roles are valid for some people in some families, they are becoming exceedingly rare and they certainly aren't the ideal roles for most people in most families. Don't assume that your role will be, or should be, exactly the same as it was in your parents' marriage or in your previous family situation. Often couples see a new marriage as a chance to change or modify family roles, and prior to the wedding you have a great opportunity to discuss the issue.

****

Sheila (34), a teacher, and Tim Smith (36), a school principal, have been married for one year. Sheila has two sons from a previous marriage, Derek (15) and Kyle (13). Tim is the father of their son Nicky (3), and daughter Jillian (6 months). They met at their church in Santa Fe, New Mexico and lived together for four years before marrying.

Sheila: *Tim and I had this really weird argument the other night. Since I just had Jilli, we decided that I should take this year off from teaching and stay home with her and Nicky. So, the other day I'd been driving the older boys to their baseball and soccer practices, with the little ones in tow, and Tim came home about five minutes after I got home. He was all put out because I hadn't made dinner! All I could think of was why is it suddenly my job to cook dinner? We always took turns before, especially on nights when the boys had sports! He actually said to me, "I'm working and you're not, so you should cook dinner." As if taking care of four kids isn't work!*

Tim: *I know it's stupid, but I guess I expected Sheila to act just like my mother because now we're married. That's what married women do – they cook dinner. And no, I never expected her to cook every night when we just lived together. I guess I thought it was different somehow.*

****

Talk about what you expect your roles to be in the family. Discuss your expectations about whether one or both of you will work outside the home, work from home or be a stay-at-home parent. What are your preferences regarding household chores and cleaning, child care, driving the kids to their activities, laundry, cooking and yard work? What about the pets – who is in charge of feeding and walking them?

David and I sort of "fell into" our roles the first year we were married. I was in seminary full-time and David worked from our home office. Since David was at home most afternoons and loves to cook, he took over the job of cooking dinner. He is more detail oriented than I am, so he does the grocery shopping and pays the bills.

Because my class and study schedule changed every few months I took on the chores that didn't have to be stringently scheduled or could be done in bits and pieces, such as laundry, vacuuming and changing the filters in the air conditioner. We discussed which household jobs we didn't mind doing and divided them up by preference. This system worked has well for us and most of the housework gets done on a regular basis. We take turns doing the jobs that neither one of us cares to do, such as cleaning the cat's litter box. Our children take turns doing the remaining chores, such as unloading the dishwasher, after their homework is done.

Expect the Best

One of the keys to successfully blending your new family is to be realistic. It's OK to be optimistic, to hope that your stepchildren will grow to love you and each other, and to pray and work hard for your family's success. However, understand that *wishing* your new stepfamily will blend instantly or *hoping* that you'll live happily ever after, may not be the most realistic way of moving into the blender. Your new family is made up of people who may be in various stages of emotional pain. In the next chapter, we'll take a look at some of the baggage that naturally comes with blending a family.

Advice from the Blender:

- Get Real! Unrealistically high expectations will only disappoint you
- Don't go nuclear
- Give it time
- Talk, talk and talk some more

Questions for reflection and discussion for the Entire Family

What are some of the things that are surprising to you about becoming a stepfamily?

What are your expectations? What are your kids' expectations? Are they unrealistic?

What are your expectations regarding:
- Finances
- Plans for the future, college for the kids, etc.
- Ex-spouses
- Family and friends
- Work and leisure time
- Household chores
- Sex and time alone
- Religion and spirituality

Are your expectations different from or similar to your spouse's?

What sort of roles do you envision in your new family? (i.e.: Who will do the laundry, cook, drive the kids to soccer, etc.) Is this different from your previous marriage? Is this deliberate?

What positive elements do you have as a family so far?

CHAPTER 2

We both have baggage … but it's cute and it matches!
Dealing with the past and making your marriage your #1 priority

"It's true we all have baggage, but if you are getting remarried you'd better make sure your baggage is one of those tiny little carry-ons, not a huge steamer trunk."

~ Rance Meyers

Due to the fact that all the members of a stepfamily didn't just magically appear in the family, we have to acknowledge that we *all* have a past. Unfortunately, one of the results of the past is emotional baggage, and having tons of unopened baggage can be deadly to a new stepfamily. So, take a deep breath and fight that urge to throw all your bags into the attic or hide them in storage. We have some unpacking to do.

Initially on life's journey, we may be carrying nothing larger than a metaphorical wallet which includes photos and memories of our family of origin, our birth order and our personality type. However, as we travel through life we pick up souvenirs from each new destination and roadside attraction along the way. Some of those souvenirs we can see, and others we can't. They may include things like childhood traumas, teenage angst, decisions – both good and bad – romantic relationships and life experiences. Often other people in our lives add souvenirs to our collections without our knowledge. As our souvenirs accumulate, we are forced to get even larger luggage to carry them. Before you know it, you may need a porter!

It will benefit you as a person, a couple and a family to unpack your individual bags and identify your souvenirs. Some of them may not be pleasant. There is probably a reason you shoved that particular souvenir to the bottom of the suitcase. Be brave – you survived the original event and you will not die by revisiting its memory years later.

Remember that your new spouse and your children *also* have baggage, and that some of their souvenirs may cause them pain. Be understanding and compassionate about this. It continues to amaze me how people can refuse to see things from other people's point of view, and can't seem to get their eyes off of themselves! You may not like that plaid shirt that your new husband has in the closet, but just because it's ugly and ripped doesn't give you the right to discard it. Ask him about it. It may have sentimental value to him. It might turn out to be the shirt he wore on the last fishing trip he took with his grandfather just before granddad passed away. Be kind and talk with your family about your baggage and your souvenirs – both the ones you see *and* the ones you don't.

Unpacking your baggage will give your family a greater understanding of each other as people, and will help all of you to be more compassionate.

So what kind of baggage are we talking about?

- **Spiritual issues**: How do you view God? Is He a loving father or angry and demanding? Why do you think you see Him this way? Do you pray?
- **Skeletons in the family closet**: Were there abusive behaviors, mental illness or addictions in your parental home? Did your parents divorce or spend years in angry silence? Were your parents like *Ozzie and Harriet,* or more like Ozzy Osbourne? What roles did you take on in your family of origin?
- **Work and career**: What did you want to be when you grew up? What are your career goals now? Have you ever been fired?
- **Emotional traumas**: Have you *fully* recovered from your divorce? Have you survived any abuse, addictions, disasters or other traumas? How do you cope with painful emotions?
- **Finances**: What does money mean to you – is it power, control or security? What does your checkbook say about you and your values?
- **Conflict and management skills**: How do you handle conflict or stress? Do you ever numb intense emotions with food, alcohol or drugs?
- **Sexuality**: Have you ever looked for love in all the wrong places or confused sex with love? Is there any sexual trauma or abuse in your past? What emotions does sexual intimacy invoke in you?

This list is by no means complete, but it will give you and your new spouse a starting point for empathetic discussion and emotional healing. Help each other with your baggage!

"We carry baggage from the past with us, no matter how desperately we'd like to leave it behind. Despite the obvious negatives (the extra weight, the drag on us, and the dysfunction baggage can produce), our inability to shake the past is a good thing in many respects. God uses the experiences, disappointments, and heartaches of the past to take us deeper in our relationship with Him. In the process, we gain wisdom and become more sensitive to the struggles of others."[5]

****

Lori (41), a stay-at-home mom, and Matt (51), an attorney, have been married for six years and live in San Diego, California. She has two children by her first marriage, a boy Taylor (16) and a girl Darcy (14). Matt had previously been married three times and has no biological children.

Lori: *Six years ago when we created this new family unit, I don't think any of us knew what was ahead. I married a man with lots of baggage. He married a woman with lots of baggage. We pull something out of our baggage on a regular basis, not quite sure what's left inside but at least we're willing to look. This is what keeps our marriage alive. That, along with counseling!*

I grew up in a family with two parents that did not love each other. I lived in fear that any day could be the day that one of them would leave. I was an adult when they finally divorced and swore I would never raise my kids in a household where the parents did not love each other. This is one of the many reasons for my divorce from the kids' dad. I only knew one thing for sure when I married Matt: we loved each other and we would be fine examples of what a loving rela-

tionship was all about. *I was going to give my kids what I didn't get, what was most important to me. I am committed to this marriage and won't go through another divorce. I adhere to my promise of keeping a household in which Matt and I love each other and we often work backwards when conflicts arise instead of fleeing under the bed! When a conflict arises I always start at where I want to be: this house of love thing. I try not to say hurtful words to the person I promised to love. I tell myself that whatever we're dealing with could be a crisis or just another event in life – the choice is mine. I want to demonstrate to my kids that conflict is normal, it happens all the time. Without it we would all be quite wishy-washy.*

Matt: *I think one of the most helpful things we stumbled upon was a book called The Five Love Languages[6]. I think we both finally understood that we all show love in a different way, just as we all feel loved in different ways. So many of our disagreements arose out of this simple misunderstanding! Lori shows love through service, and she feels loved through service done by others.*

Lori: *For example: the time Matt spends writing me a love note and leaving it in my purse makes me feel loved way more than a new diamond ring would. Matt shows love by giving material things, and he feels loved through physical contact. Anyway, this can really cause disruption in our marriage if we aren't aware of how we are showing our love to each other. We are continually working on this stuff, and I am finally realizing my most important dream is coming true; that of having a healthy marriage.*

****

When looking at your baggage you may have to go all the way back to the beginning. David and I lived in the same suburban town in Massachusetts and met when we were 12 years old, on the first day of seventh grade. We had each moved to town that summer, although neither of us knew the other was also "a new kid". We were best friends all through junior high and high school. We even attended the prom together, although with separate dates. I never liked any of the girls David went out with; they weren't good enough for him, in my opinion. He wasn't fond of the guys I dated either, but it never occurred to us to date each other.

We grew up in very similar homes. We were both the oldest in our families. Our parents were professionals who attended Protestant churches, sang in the choir or served on the board, and insisted that we attend the youth group. David's parents hosted cocktail parties; my parents instituted a daily happy hour. Same song, different house.

The old adage that opposites attract proved itself in both of our first marriages. I married an outspoken bull rider from Texas; David married an outspoken doctor from Peru. My marriage deteriorated after 12 years, due in part to my recovery from alcoholism and in part to his abusive behavior. David's marriage deteriorated after 12 years as well. We both discovered that opposites may attract initially, but even exotic gets old after a while.

After my divorce I decided that I would be content to be single for the rest of my life. The thought of dating was just too scary with young children to consider. I worked on really getting to know myself and God. However, just in case God decided to bring someone into my life, I made a list of 20 qualities I wanted in a man; mostly as a challenge, since I didn't see any one person having all of these characteristics. My list included the following: must be a committed Christian, love children, be a professional, physically fit, appreciate the arts as well as hockey, a good cook, financially responsible, intelligent, like to travel, helpful around the house, kind and compassionate … you get the idea. David had every single characteristic on the list.

Marriage was God's idea[7] and should never be entered into lightly; therefore stepcouples must address and discuss their individual relationships with God, *especially* if they come from different religious backgrounds. Agreement in the spiritual department is vital, especially when children are involved. This is not simply a matter of if you will attend church and if so which one. Spiritual issues can undermine a marriage, and the enemy of our souls would like nothing better than to disrupt your marriage before it even begins. As believers, you need to really grasp the fact that God forgives all of your sins, including the sins that brought about your divorce. And, divorce is *not* an unforgivable sin!

No matter what your religious background, it's not uncommon to feel a stigma about becoming a stepfamily. This is frequently a self-forgiveness issue, and couples should pray *together* over their new marriage and ask God's forgiveness for their past mistakes. Once you realize that you are both forgiven and that God still loves you, you can move forward and pray for the Lord's blessing for your future together as a family. It also doesn't hurt to remember that Jesus grew up in a stepfamily[8]!

Other major areas that you will need to address and fully discuss include stepfamily role expectations, individual family histories (both your families of origin and your prior marriages), your sexual histories, your individual financial situations, and your personality and communication styles. Complete openness and honesty is the best strategy for your marriage. It may feel awkward and embarrassing to be completely open about your past, but your marriage and your family will be stronger for it.

We recommend that stepcouples take individual personality inventories[9] and discuss their results together to help them become aware of their similarities and differences, potential areas of conflict, and effective ways to communicate with each other. Read at least one book together about strengthening your marriage and at least one book on stepparenting. Discuss what you read and find ways you can put any newly learned skills into practice.

****

Kelly (35) and Randy (45) have been married for two years. They live in Charleston, South Carolina and are both employed by a large Christian church. Randy's first marriage lasted 13 years, and he has full custody of his two daughters, Brooke (15) and Amber (12). This is Kelly's first marriage. She had two previous live-in relationships, and no biological children.

Kelly: *We are probably not your typical stepfamily. I met Randy's girls first when I was their Sunday school teacher. I watched them go through the painful breakup of their parents, and saw how that affected them, before Randy and I ever even considered having a relationship with each other.*

Randy: *I was the pastor for adult singles in our church and right after my divorce part of the curriculum I was teaching became really relevant to me on a personal level. I let the Holy Spirit lead me through my own recovery from the divorce. I also was really attracted to the idea of biblical courtship as opposed to dating, so when Kelly came into my life, that seemed like the perfect way for us to go. We courted for a year before we married.*

Kelly: *Biblical courtship involves "front-loading" your relationship. We talked about everything: our goals in life, our pasts, every issue we could imagine. It is all about balancing your emotions, your spirit, the physical aspects of your life, and being accountable to someone else outside of your relationship. We built our relationship on a foundation of friendship first. Then we literally listed everything we wanted in our marriage together – our family life, our* *hobbies, practical stuff like who does the laundry or the cooking. We read books and we went to a marriage counselor before we were even married. Our counselor told us that we were more compatible than couples he'd seen who'd been married for years.*

Randy: *We talked and prayed and talked through that whole year. We waited for marriage, as far as the physical stuff. Our first kiss on the lips was at our wedding and while it may be unconventional by today's standards, it was definitely worth the wait.*

Kelly: *It's never too late to ask for forgiveness and reclaim your purity.*

****

Shared Intimacy

It is important to share your family and sexual histories, and discuss them together or share them on paper. By examining your pasts together, you can identify and sort out potential areas of contention. This sharing exercise is vitally important because not only will it help you to forgive and move beyond the past, it will also engender empathy and strengthen your commitment to each other. It's also a great idea to discuss your sexual expectations for your marriage, even if it's uncomfortable at first. Acknowledging what your own sexual needs are, and discussing how you can meet each other's needs is vital to a healthy marriage. Talk about how frequently you would like to be intimate. If your relationship in the bedroom is healthy, loving and satisfying, the rest of your relationship will benefit.

Part of the reason that second marriages fail at a greater rate than first marriages is that people tend to rush into new relationships *without healing the pain of their past relationships first*. We have seen this time and again as stepfamilies are torn apart by recidivistic divorce. Ron Deal, author of *The Smart Stepfamily*, notes that many remarriages are haunted by what he calls "the ghost of marriage past[10]." Therefore, it is very beneficial to devote considerable time exploring what caused the problems in your first marriages, whether it was lack of marital communication, your personal avoidance styles, poor conflict resolution skills or abusive behaviors. Any of these could evolve into emotional triggers that will affect your new marriage if you do not deal with them up front. Don't repeat the same mistakes. Learn what you can from the errors of the past.

****

It was 6 months before their wedding that Sheila realized she owed it to Tim to tell him about her past.

Tim: *I knew that Sheila had a nasty divorce – our first date was on the same day her divorce was final – but I had no idea that she grew up in an alcoholic and abusive family. It was very hard for her to share that, and it was really hard to hear, but I'm really glad she did so now I understand why she hates conflict so much, and why she acts the way she does sometimes.*

Sheila: *It was really hard for me to talk to Tim, but it helped him see that I'm not crazy. I hate arguing for a reason. I'm terrified of yelling, because in my family when my Dad was drinking it always led to yelling and physical abuse for my Mom, my sister and me. This was one of the things that broke up my first marriage. Well ... that and I married a guy just like my Dad. I never made the connection until recently, but I finally figured out that when I sense conflict I bail. I'm learning that it's OK to disagree with someone, and that it doesn't mean that the relationship has to end or that it will get violent.*

Anyway, about six months before our wedding I realized that Tim and I never talked about anything, let alone the past! We never discussed our living arrangements – he just moved in when I found out I was pregnant with Nicky. Then we didn't talk about getting married until I got pregnant with Jilli. He said "I guess we should get married, huh?" It wasn't much of a proposal, but I guess it was something.

Tim: *It's ironic. My brother is a pastor, but he told us that we were already married in God's eyes, and I wanted to believe him. But when Sheila got pregnant the second time I felt really guilty. I felt like we needed to stop and do things differently.*

Sheila: *We realized that we were sinning [by living together], and that we needed to change that. Not talking about it wouldn't make it go away, and we weren't setting a good example for our kids. So we went to the pastor of our church and admitted that we weren't married, but we wanted to be. He worked with us and prayed with us a lot. I learned that if you're in sin, God can't bless you. But if you change what you're doing, He can forgive you and bless you[11]. And He has. We're much happier now that we've gotten married. Better late than never.*

****

It is essential that you tackle the issue of communication, not only with respect to the past but also as a strategic and proactive characteristic of your new marriage. Dr. John Gottman, the leading researcher in the field of strategic communication, has analyzed reasons behind marriage failures. His research indicates that things like criticism, contempt, defensiveness and withdrawal are incredibly damaging to communication in marriage[12]. As part of a proactive strategy, specifically plan ways to avoid these negative behaviors in your new marriage.

While the goal for your new marriage may be "it won't be anything like my first marriage" it helps to have more specific objectives in mind. Your top priority should be your own personal growth – to become a mature, emotionally intelligent person, preferably before you marry. According to Dr. Mavis Hetherington, a researcher in the field of divorce and remarriage, "The most important factor in the success of a second marriage is the choice of a mature, stable supportive spouse with good problem-solving skills. A stable partner can help a spouse learn to be more self-controlled, sensitive and constructive in dealing with problems that inevitably arise in a stepfamily[13]." Instead of looking for the right person, *be* the right person!

Money

Discussing and planning for financial harmony is difficult enough in any marriage, but when one considers the additional impact that alimony and/or child support has on a couple, money becomes even more contentious for blending families. There is no one right way to handle stepfamily finances, but honest communication and flexibility are crucial.

Whether you choose to pool your finances or keep separate "his, hers and ours" accounts, it is important that you agree on the basics of money management. This includes: the household budget, who pays for what, the record-keeping system and who pays the bills, debt and the use of credit cards, discretionary funds and how often you will discuss financial matters as a couple.

Honesty is the best policy, so *fully* disclose your complete financial histories to one another, including whether you've been through a personal bankruptcy, which can impact your financial profile for ten years or more. Be sure to discuss things like any existing trusts or wills you might have, insurance policies and beneficiaries, debts, retirement accounts, college funds for the children, and investments.

Non-Nuclear Proliferation Treaties or Prenuptial Agreements

You should decide whether or not a prenuptial agreement is right for you as a couple, and how you will plan for your – and your children's – financial futures. It may help to view a prenuptial agreement as a financial plan for your future together, rather than a plan of action in case the marriage doesn't work out.

****

Lori: *We met through a surprise 'set up' by some mutual friends who thought it would be interesting to see if "Mr. Gucci" and "Ms. Granola" could make things work! I came to this marriage with nothing: I had two kids and four jobs which barely allowed me to make ends meet. Matt came to this marriage having lost half of all his stuff three different times. Upon deciding to marry, I was presented with a prenup. Matt set up an appointment with a lawyer for me to go over everything, but I was fuming. I took it very personally, as a jab at my character. However, I tried to see it from his point of view and thought, "if half of all I had earned was taken away every five or six years, what would I do?" I signed it and have never looked at it again.*

Matt: *Lori and I think very differently in regards to finance and property: I like to know where every penny goes. She is more of a "free spirit" when it comes to spending and saving.*

Lori: *I am not an ignorant woman who lets the man handle the finances entirely, but I just have no interest in knowing all the details. I am very grateful for what we have* *and the fact that Matt likes to handle the money. In the fourth year of our marriage, my name was added to our checking account. Up until then, Matt would write me a check for cash whenever I needed something. Some people would probably have a problem with that, but I didn't. I decided that I was not going to allow money to be the puppet master of my life.*

****

Even if one of you is a financial genius, take the time to read one or two books on finances together. Contact a financial counselor if you find that you need more in-depth financial counseling. Money is one of those areas that will continually need your attention throughout your marriage, and it's best to begin with both of you on the same page and with a solid plan.

We're Number One!

Because stepfamilies form backwards – at least one of you was a parent *before* you became a couple – the most important thing you can do is to make your marriage your number one priority, *especially* if you already have children.[14] All of the leading stepfamily advocates agree that stepcouples must commit to making their marriage as strong as possible. This may sound like common sense, but in the daily chaos of a stepfamily, the marriage is something that can easily become unprioritized.

- Pray for and with each other daily. Thank God for your spouse.
- Seek out God's purpose and plan for your marriage.[15]
- Put a lock on your bedroom door – and use it!

- Go out on a date with each other (no kids) every week or two. Make this a non-negotiable priority and write it on your calendars in ink.
- Find a hobby that you can share: take walks together; take up scuba diving, ballroom dancing or mountain biking; start a garden; join a gym; build birdhouses; get season tickets to the opera, theater or local college basketball games; join a recreational adult kickball team or a bowling league. Whatever you choose, find something to do *together* that you both enjoy!
- Write down all of the romantic things you and your partner do for each other, and make a point to keep doing these things.
- Surprise your spouse with a gift or card that expresses your love.
- Think of little things your spouse would appreciate and do them (for example: make her a cup of coffee; do the laundry even if it's his turn).
- Send flowers just because (men like to get flowers too).
- Call from work to say "I love you".
- Commit to spending 30 minutes together every evening just talking, without the TV, phone, computer or kids as distractions.
- Have a "No TV in the bedroom" policy.
- Each year take a vacation or at least a weekend away as a couple (no kids!) Think of it as a yearly honeymoon.

Marry One, Get One or More Free!

At the same time you are trying to make your new marriage your first priority, you must also consider your children's and/or stepchildren's needs. Children in a blended family are part of the package deal that you signed up for when you decided to marry your spouse. Unfortunately, they are also one of the reasons that stepfamilies fail to blend. In the next chapter, we will examine what it means to suddenly find yourself in an instant family, and how this influences the blending process.

Advice from the Blender:

- Unpack *all* of your baggage!
- Get counseling if you need it
- Honesty is the best policy
- Become the best person you can be
- Make your marriage your #1 priority

Questions for reflection and discussion for You and Your New Spouse

What brought you together in the first place and what made you decide to get married?

What obstacles have you already overcome?

Have you dealt with your past? Has your spouse dealt with his/her past?

How have you dealt with each other's pasts, previous marriages, families of origin, etc.?

How open and honest have you been with each other? Now is the time to come clean!

Discuss your wants and needs in the following areas, and rank them in order of priority:
- Spirituality
- Recreation and hobbies
- Time: me, us, family
- Intellectual pursuits
- Music, the arts, sports
- Work and careers
- Parenting styles
- Roles in the family/household: housework, cooking, etc.
- Love languages
- Finances
- Conflict management
- Sex
- Other areas that are important to you

Advice From The Blender

How is your spiritual life? Can you begin praying together?

What can you do to make your marriage #1? List three things to put into practice.

CHAPTER 3

The Package Deal
Bonding as a family without resorting to Superglue or duct tape

◎

"You don't choose your family. They are God's gift to you, as you are to them."
> ~ Bishop Desmond Tutu

When David and I married, we made a commitment to each other *and* to each other's children. We both understood that we got a package deal when we got married. I arrived at this marriage with two kids, two dogs and a hamster. David arrived with two kids and a cat. I vowed to love and accept them all into our family, even though I'm not a "cat person". David did the same. I was, and still am, uncomfortable calling Lysa or Chase my stepchildren, because it made them seem like they were somehow *less than* my other two. We decided that neither of us had just two children anymore – we both had four. We refer to all of them as *our* children.

Advice From The Blender

David explains it this way: "Susan and I made the commitment to raise all of these kids together. We try to treat them the same, love them the same. Some days it's not easy, but the Lord gave them to us to raise, and we just look at it like they are all gifts from God. We are privileged to be able to take care of them."

This can be difficult if, for example, a non-custodial parent is only involved with the children sporadically. This type of situation calls for an extra dose of compassion on the part of parents and stepparents, and a conscious decision not to cry foul (at least, not out loud). Raising kids is not about YOU. Keep in mind that God chose you – as a couple – to parent these children. It doesn't matter if their other parents choose to be involved or not. When the kids are in your home they are yours. We look at our situation like this: we have four children all the time and sometimes they visit their other parents.

So how are you supposed to "bond" as a stepfamily? Here are some ideas:

- **Dinner time:** Eat family dinners together as often as possible, with all members of the family who happen to be in the house that day. This gets increasingly difficult as children grow into teenagers with extracurricular activities and social lives, but keep the tradition as often as you can. If dinners are impossible, eat breakfast together.
- **Make a date:** Use a color-coded calendar system or day planner. Pick one colored pen or marker for each member of the family, and only use that color to write in their activities on the calendar. For instance, in my calendar Zonie's activities are written in red, Tanner's in blue, Lysa's in green, Chase's in orange, etc. Keep one master calendar in a very visible place, perhaps posted in the

kitchen. This way everyone in the family can see what everyone else is doing, what is planned and which activities everyone is expected to attend.
- **Be a soccer mom or dad:** Support each child's extracurricular activities. If possible the entire family should attend important games, performances and recitals. Over the past few years David and I have logged thousands of hours at soccer practices, guitar and drum lessons, and theatre rehearsals. By encouraging our children to pursue their passions, we have also built strong family bonds. Granted, sometimes it is difficult to get the other kids to attend their siblings' activities without grumbling, but it means the world to "the star" when their whole family is there cheering them on!
- **Take a vacation:** One of the things we did immediately was commit to taking a family vacation every year. By "family" I mean David, myself and all four of our kids. We are lucky enough to live in Scottsdale, Arizona where the school system has a weeklong fall break, as well as the better-known spring break. The fall break has become our family vacation week. Each year we go somewhere for a week of "forced family fun". One year we visited theme parks in California, the following year we rented a beach house, and one year we took a four-night cruise to Mexico. The kids have all loved the vacations, it has given us all a chance to get to know each another in a more relaxed atmosphere, and it gives us all something to look forward to every year. It is one of our *new* family traditions.
- **Take the weekend off:** If a weeklong vacation is not possible, be deliberate about taking week-

end mini-vacations and bonding around attractions in your own town or state. Tour a museum together, go to a movie, play in the park, go bowling or miniature golfing, or stay at home and have a family game night. We have taken family weekend trips to various locations in and around Arizona: hiking in the Grand Canyon, rafting on the Colorado River, exploring caves at Kartchner Caverns, touring a mine in Bisbee. What natural attractions are waiting for your family in your state?

- **Movie nights:** Start a Friday night tradition of pizza and DVDs. All family members take turns choosing the movie that everyone watches. (And no complaining if you have to sit through *The Little Mermaid* for the tenth time).
- **Ask questions:** Get to know your stepchildren: who are their friends, what kind of music do they like, what's their favorite color, what kind of food do they love, what is their favorite sport and TV show, what is the name of the stuffed critter they sleep with, who is their hero, what are their best and worst subjects in school, what is their secret talent, what do they want to be when they grow up? Ask and find out.
- **Matinees:** Bail all of the kids out of school one afternoon and go to a movie. If you go early enough you'll get the discounted matinee rate, and the kids will think you are cool for getting them out of school early (obviously, this should be a very rare event).
- **"Date" your stepkids:** Spend some one-on-one time together. Take them out for lunch, take a walk or play together in the backyard. This will allow you to get to know each other without the

pressure of having their parent and other siblings around.

You Can't Argue With a House

Discipline is a major source of conflict in stepfamilies. In fact, it is such a common issue that it is ranked as one of the top three concerns for stepfamilies entering therapy[16].

Parents may find that they have opposing disciplinary styles (authoritative/permissive), or they may have unconscious fears about letting the stepparent discipline the children at all. Couples need to talk about discipline in general, and come to an agreement as to what the behavioral expectations and discipline will look like in their home. The wisest way to handle this matter is for the couple to discuss it honestly *before* it becomes an issue.

****

Lori: *Although I wanted Matt to be every bit the children's new Dad, I found myself resentful when he tried to discipline them. Taylor was usually the one needing discipline – he's our defiant child. I rarely voiced an opinion when our styles clashed because either (1) Matt was doing the best he could, so who was I to tell him he wasn't handling things right? Or, (2) I didn't know how to handle it myself because I was afraid of making a mistake. Our parenting styles were not discussed before we got married since Matt didn't have kids, and to be honest, I don't even think I had a consistent one in place.*

Matt: *Lori's ex-husband's new wife had no kids of her own either, but according to Taylor and Darcy, she was never happy with their behavior. She often said that if they were her kids, they would not be "this way" – whatever that means. Basically the poor kids suddenly had four parents* *and four completely different parenting styles to figure out. Our parental circle consisted of one angry controller, one screamer, one analyzing lecturer and one scatterbrained, smothering guilt-ridden person. And we thought all we needed was love – HA!*

****

Tom Wheeler of the Changing Families ministry in South Carolina says: "I disagree with the current thought that only a biological parent can discipline a child. This, in my experience, causes a divisive line that can only result in double standards that kids will resent. You end up trying to maintain two families under one roof and a house divided against itself. Response to infractions should be decided [upon] in private by both adults[17]."

****

Sheila: *Discipline was one of those areas that we just never talked about. I guess I figured that since Tim was a teacher and a school principal, he'd know how to discipline kids. However, when he moved in with us, I noticed that every time my boys would act up, he'd come get me and tell me to handle it. As Nicky became a toddler and started getting into things, I noticed Tim would do the same thing with him! He just kept delegating the discipline to me. We recently talked about it, and Tim didn't even realize he was doing it. He's now taking a more hands-on approach with all the boys.*

****

David and I sat down and discussed the whole subject of discipline privately, then agreed upon and wrote down 10 behavioral expectations for our children, along with accompanying consequences for violating those expectations. Together, we presented "The Rules of Our Home" to all of the kids during a family meeting shortly after we married. We discussed exactly what we expected of them and why, and the consequences that would occur should they choose to break the rules. Our rules were fairly simple:

- We treat everyone with respect, kindness and love.
- We use our manners *all* the time.
- We do not call each other names, say "shut up", or cuss.
- We do not hit.
- We ask permission before using other people's stuff.
- We do what a parent asks, when they ask.
- We understand what "No" means.
- We tell someone where we are going when we leave the house.
- We do not throw things or play ball in the house.
- We only eat and drink in the kitchen.

By working on a discipline plan together and presenting it to the children as a united front, the kids got the message that these were *the house rules* – as opposed to my rules or his rules. A child can't argue with a house. By implementing this system, we also avoided the inevitable stepchild announcement of "you can't tell me what to do because you're not my Mom/Dad."

Consequences range from time outs for the younger children to loss of privileges (like TV or computer time) for the older children. We keep the rules posted on the refrigerator, and this system has been successful for our family. We update the rules when necessary, dropping rules that no longer seem necessary and adding new ones as the situation dictates. And as the kids have gotten older we have found it effective to have them choose their own consequences. They are usually harder on themselves than we would be. However, we have also found that we have to periodically refresh the kids' memories about what the rules *really* say; for instance: "We do what a parent asks, *when* they ask," still does not have an exception clause.

****

Rob (45), a former NFL player and president of a large corporation, and Kendra (41), an accountant, live in a suburb of Seattle. They have been married for five years and both have two teenagers. Kendra's girls are Leah (17) and Kara (16) and Rob's children are Kristy (16) and Eric (15).

Rob: *You just haven't lived until you have four teenagers under the same roof!*

Kendra: *Our major problems weren't just that we had teenagers, but that we also had completely different parenting styles. Rob is an imposing guy and he's very by-the-book – very strict. I'm much more laid back. However, my two girls live with us full time, and Rob really only saw his kids on weekends, so ironically, he was a much more lax with his kids than he was with mine. All four of the kids quickly learned to play us off each other! It was absolutely insane for the first few years or so.*

Rob: *It didn't help that I was on the road a lot that first year. Kendra had to deal with a lot of this on her own. My kids figured out how to get away with crap fast – if I was out of town on business they just ran all over Kendra. And it just got worse as they got older. We ended up sending Eric to boarding school last year because he was so out of control.*

Kendra: *I keep thinking that the situation could have turned us against each other and ruined our marriage, but* *we got counseling and worked through a lot of these issues. The discipline issue turned out to be just a symptom of some deeper things the kids were going through.*

Rob: *Part of it was that we had to learn to think like a team, which we didn't do for the first few years.*

****

The Sex Talk

Imagine you are having dinner with your in-laws in a nice restaurant and your seven-year-old loudly asks "What's oral sex?" This is a good indication that it's time to have the sex talk.

This is one of those areas which can wreak havoc in a stepfamily, mainly because nobody anticipates it. As parental partners, discuss with each other – and with the other parents if possible – when, and in how much detail, you will talk to your children about sex. Discuss with each other about how open *you* are to talking with the kids, and who will handle the discussion. Don't assume your children's other parent will be rushing to have the sex talk with the kids, but don't assume that they won't. You might be surprised to find out what the children pick up from their other parents, stepparents or older siblings. This is also a good time to install a lock on your bedroom door as a precaution against unexpected visitors in the night – you don't want your child's education in sexuality to begin with a visually shocking incident.

Talk to the kids together – the earlier the better. Answer the questions honestly whenever a child asks. Never say "go ask your mother/father" because this just puts undue strain on an already shaky relationship and adds to the confusion. Some children find it more comfortable to discuss sex with a stepparent – they seem to sense less judgmental pressure there.

Don't wait until the kids begin asking questions. You might not think that they are old enough to understand the concept of sex, but when you get remarried the children *will* notice that you are no longer sleeping alone. Older kids will automatically leap to the conclusion that you are ... (gasp!) ...having sex! A perfect opportunity to bring up the subject of sexual relations in marriage, morality and boundaries may be just prior to the wedding.

David and I did not live together before we got married, but since we were living in separate states, he technically moved into our house two weeks prior to our wedding. I was already planning to discuss this arrangement with my children, but Zonie wasted no time in bringing it up. As soon as his furniture arrived she asked, "Where is David going to sleep?"

"In the office, on the sofa." I answered.

"Why isn't he going to sleep in your room?"

"Because we aren't married yet," I said. "He'll move into our room after our wedding."

"But Daddy and ____ lived together and slept in the same room before they got married," she countered.

"I know, Sweetie. That was their choice. And our choice is to wait until we are married."

The topic of sexuality must also include proper dating and friendship guidelines for your kids as they become teenagers. Keep in mind that when you and your spouse got married, you became related to one another and while it may be a fuzzier distinction; your children are considered *siblings* – even if the official term is stepsiblings. It should go without saying that boundaries must be created to prevent incestuous sexual contact between stepsiblings, as well as between stepparents and stepchildren. Unfortunately, unless that boundary is *clearly* defined, children and young teens may not understand the implications. We are aware of one situation in which teenaged stepsiblings became intimately involved with each other and the result was heartbreaking.

Slug Stew and a Vegetable

One of the best ways to combat unrealistic expectations and bond as a family is to have a sense of humor. Life does not have to be deadly serious all the time, even in a stepfamily. No matter what situation your new family finds itself in, look for something humorous or silly about it, and start a collection of funny stories and inside family jokes.

****

Kara (16): *The funniest thing that happened to us was like the third year we were all together. It was Thanksgiving, and everyone was arguing about what we were going to eat. In our family we always had a gigantic turkey with potatoes and pie and stuff, but in Rob's family Thanksgiving wasn't a big deal because he used to play football and usually wasn't home. So we were all yelling, making suggestions and fighting about what we should eat for Thanksgiving and Mom says in this absolutely serious tone that she's going to cook slug stew and some sort of vegetable. There was like this deadly silence for about a minute and then everyone busted up laughing.*

****

Sloane: *One time during a family dinner, Cassidy and Cole were bickering about whose turn it was to clear the table, Alisha and Thatcher were bickering over something else, and I was at my wit's end when suddenly Jason starts singing a song from The Simpson's… "fight, fight, fight…fight, fight, fight…it's the Itchy & Scratchy show…" in this really* *high squeaky voice. At that exact moment, Cassidy spilled her milk all over her plate, and Cole, who had just taken a drink of his milk, started laughing and sprayed everyone at the table with milk ... it was just absolutely absurd!*

****

Monica (25) a stay-at-home Mom, and Steve (37) a Casino executive, were married a little more than a year ago and live in Las Vegas, Nevada. Monica's son, Cameron (5), lives with them full-time and occasionally sees his father on weekends. Steve's two daughters, Lindy (8) and Hailey (10), divide their time equally between their mother and father, alternating homes every other week.

Steve: *One evening my girls were supposed to be clearing the table after dinner, but they were completely rambunctious, just being silly and not getting anything cleaned up at all. Monica stormed into the kitchen and the girls froze, like they were expecting to get into trouble, but instead of yelling at them Monica started chasing them around the kitchen like she was Dracula. Both the girls ran screaming out of the kitchen, laughing hysterically.*

****

Remember that laughter is the best medicine, but not when it is hurtful to someone else. Do not allow anyone in the family to cruelly tease another or use someone as a scapegoat. Keep your sense of humor light and self-deprecating. Always build one another up and speak well of each other.

The key to bonding as a blended family is to *choose* to love your new family members. You got a package deal – marry one, get one (or more) free! Make the decision and the effort to love them all.

The Wicked Stepmother Syndrome

We won't sugar-coat it: choosing to love, and live with, children who wish you were dead is not easy. There are no magic words which will speed up a developing stepchild/stepparent relationship. There are no mysterious potions that will make them love you. However, there are ways to build relationships with your stepchildren that don't involve magic mirrors, glass slippers or poisoned apples. We will explore some of those in the following chapter.

Advice from the Blender:

- A house divided cannot stand
- No one plans to fail – they fail to plan
- Have fun! Enjoy one another as a family. Have a sense of humor
- Have a discipline plan worked out before behavior becomes an issue
- Discuss and set boundaries within the family
- Be kind to one another
- CHOOSE to love ALL your family members

Questions for Reflection and Discussion for the Entire Family

How will the transition work: whose house will you live in, will bedrooms be shared, how will you help your family to adjust?

Have you discussed discipline and behavior expectations?

Can you answer the following questions about your children and stepchildren?
- Who are their friends?
- What kind of music do they like?
- What's their favorite color?
- What kind of food do they love?
- What is their favorite sport and sports team?
- What is the name of the stuffed critter they sleep with?
- Who is their hero?
- What are their best and worst subjects in school?
- What is their secret talent?
- What do they want to be when they grow up?

Have you discussed privacy issues and your own personal boundaries? What about those of the children?

What about new vs. old traditions – what traditions will your family keep, what new traditions will you start?

List three specific things you plan to do to help the family bond. How can you put these into practice?

Do you have any funny family stories yet?

CHAPTER 4

The Infiltrator …
and other names for stepparents
Helping the kids adjust

"I think Cinderella's stepmother was just stressed out and seriously misunderstood."

~ *Anonymous*

To children, the birth of a stepfamily is a death-sentence to their fantasy that mom and dad will get back together someday. From everything we've learned about the effects of divorce on children, we know that this is a *very* real desire for almost all kids whose parents divorce[18]. It doesn't matter how bad the first marriage was or how old the kids were when their parents split up. Children persistently cling to this fantasy.

****

Jason: *Cole wasn't even 2 years old when I moved out of my first wife's house. He surprised us one day, two years after my wedding to Sloane, when he said, "I want things back the way they were when you and Mommy lived in the same house and everyone was happy." I don't think he actually remembers when I lived in that house ... and believe me, nobody was happy!*

****

The reality of mom and dad never getting back together becomes horribly clear to a child when one of their parents marries someone else. This results in feelings of confusion, anger and grief in the child. Children are rarely able to verbalize these feelings, and in fact may not even be aware of them. Often these emotions are acted out with temper tantrums, academic failure, and anti-social or aggressive behavior, depending on the child's age. The children's behavior is such a common issue that it is ranked as another of the top three concerns for stepfamilies entering therapy[19].

Shortly after my marriage to David, my son Tanner began to bring home D's on his schoolwork instead of the A's and B's he was capable of. I assumed he was having trouble adjusting to his new school because we moved from Las Vegas to Arizona, but in a counseling session he admitted that he was angry with me for getting married. He wanted David "to just disappear". It was difficult for him to talk about those feelings, and he felt very conflicted because on the one hand he actually likes David, but he also didn't want to "share Mom with another guy".

Remember that children often deal with strong emotions in bits and pieces over time. For example, when a child's parents divorce, he or she may not acknowledge or even feel the grief until two or more years after the divorce. The child may pretend that nothing has changed, and act as if the divorce doesn't bother them at all. Or they may act out sporadically with alternating periods of anger, sadness and happiness. When one of the parents remarries, the child's grief over the divorce may intensify when combined with anger over the new marriage. All of these strong emotions may manifest themselves in behavioral problems which *seem* to have no rational connection to any precipitating event. Counselors often refer to children exhibiting these behaviors as "sleeper children".

****

Jennifer: *My kids reacted quite differently. Alexa was always an easygoing girl. At least, that is what we thought until a few years ago when she found her voice and it was a really angry voice. For five years she just quietly went along with what we did. Then she suddenly lashed out and destroyed her bedroom at her dad's house! We were shocked – we had all thought she was fine with the divorce and my remarriage. We got her into counseling just so she could work through the feelings that were buried for so long. She is doing much better now.*

Sasha was the openly defiant one. I use the word defiant because he was actually the scapegoat we all focused on. In reality, he was the one who faced things head on when we adults weren't being honest about this fantasy life we all thought we were living. He is an observer. He learned where all our buttons were, where the loopholes were and he used them to his advantage. He challenged everything and exhausted everyone. In retrospect, he was the only one without the rose-colored glasses on. I realize now that the kids each grieved in their own ways, but neither reaction was easy to deal with.

****

Hurting People Hurt Other People

The anger and grief that the children feel may also emerge on holidays or on the anniversaries of either the divorce or their parents' remarriages – essentially, any occasion that could have emotional connotations. We noticed this phenomenon with my daughter Zonie just this past year. She became moody and irritable in early November, around the anniversary of her father's remarriage. Her mood continued for two weeks into the Thanksgiving holiday. When her father failed to call her on Thanksgiving Day she became openly hostile to everyone in our house; slamming doors, stomping around and yelling at all of us.

That weekend I bought her a new pair of jeans, and within the hour she had "customized" them with a Sharpie pen and a pair of scissors. Normally I wouldn't object to her decorating her jeans, but she chose to write profanities all over them – using words I would never allow to be used in our home.

Zonie and I sat down and discussed her unacceptable behavior and attitude – or should I say, I discussed; she glared. After many tears (both hers and mine), I suggested to her that many children of divorce become angry at their absent parent but take it out on those around them. I asked her if this might be what she was going through. She came to the conclusion that maybe she was angry with her father – not our family. Once she realized this, it was as if the floodgates opened. She told me she was angry at her dad for getting remarried, for being absent from her life, and for not calling her on Thanksgiving. She was also afraid to be openly angry at him because deep down she was worried that he would disappear from her life forever. It was "easier" for her to take her anger out on our family because we were "safe". She knew that we would never leave her or reject her, no matter how atrocious and unacceptable her behavior was.

Advice From The Blender

As difficult as this situation was to deal with at the time, I am grateful that we were able to discuss the underlying issues and get to the root of the problem. Since our discussion, her attitude and behavior have been wonderful. If we had not addressed her emotions – her anger as well as her fears – her behavior might have spiraled out of control.

Being Displaced

A further problem for children involves their place in the family. Birth orders become muddied when families blend. The baby of the family may suddenly find herself the middle child, with younger, cuter kids competing for the attention that used to be exclusively hers. Likewise, mom's older son may suddenly lose his place as the "man of the house" and dad's only daughter may find that she is no longer "the princess". Finding their place in a blending family is very difficult for children, and unless they can talk about their feelings they may think that they are the only confused one in the family. It is absolutely vital to talk about these feelings with your children.

****

Karen (38), a bank manager, and Jon (33), a police officer, have been married for seven years. They live in central Texas. Karen shares custody of her daughter Mandy (13) with her ex-husband, and Jon shares custody of his daughter, Ariel (9) with his ex-wife. Five years ago Karen and Jon had a son, Dylan. Their family expanded again last fall with the sudden death of Jon's brother. Jon and Karen became the legal guardians for Jon's teenage nephews, Steven (16) and Daniel (14).

Mandy (13): *When my parents were married to each other, I was an only child. When my dad got married he and my stepmom had a baby right away, so I was the big sister. My mom got married to Jon that same year. He already had Ariel and then they had Dylan. In two years I went from being an only child to being the oldest of four kids. Then last year our cousins came to live with us and my dad and stepmom had another baby, so now I'm the third kid in the middle of seven! It sucks. Sometimes I don't know who I am.*

****

This confusion is not only about their own place in the family but the positions of others as well. Questions may arise like:

- Is it OK if I call him my brother, not my stepbrother?
- Can you divorce your kids too?
- What about their grandparents - are they my grandparents too?
- They aren't really my sisters – why do we have to be nice?
- Does this mean that we have step-cousins?
- Why do I have to do what she says – she's not my Mom!

Answering their questions in a neutral setting prior to the marriage will help the children adjust to their impending new roles, and help them understand that they are not the only ones feeling confused.

Pieces of Pie

It is also imperative to assure children that it is OK if they *do not love* their stepparent or stepsiblings right away.

Love is never instantaneous, it develops over time. It is very important to assure the children that no one is going to *force* them to love their new family members. It will be enough if they can be respectful and give one another a chance. Relationships must be allowed to grow in their own time.

****

Alisha (14): *I told my Mom not to try to push me to like my stepdad cuz it took me years to even start to like my stepmom. And I think all stepparents should butt out about some issues, like if kids are allowed to date, because it's not their business.*

****

Thatcher (12): *Having a younger stepbrother and sharing a room with him sucks cuz he snores and talks and talks and talks and is really annoying. But sometimes he can be fun. Sometimes.*

****

On the other hand, some children may need to be given permission to like their new stepparent, and be assured that by liking the stepparent they are not betraying their biological parent. This is a major fear of many kids – that they will have to "choose" one person over the other. We were surprised to learn that this was true of David's son, Chase. Learning that people have enough love and affection to go around is a difficult concept for many children. Many kids think of love as being like a pie with only eight or 10 pieces. If all the pieces are allotted – to parents, siblings, grandparents, their best friend, the dog, a teddy bear, etc. – then there aren't any more pieces left to give out. They may believe that if they love their mom they would have to take her piece of pie away in order to love their stepmother. All children eventually learn that love is infinitely expandable, and there is always enough in their hearts for more people to love, but they may have to be told in simple terms and be allowed to let love develop gradually.

****

Darcy (14): *I don't like my stepmom. She thinks everything's her business, wants everyone to focus on her and she's like, controlling. She thinks everything she does is perfect and it's her way or no way. She like insisted we 'be nice' to her all the time, right away. My stepdad is the complete opposite from stepmom. I like him. I was happy when Mom married him because he's cool. He didn't like force us to be nice to him or anything.*

****

Amber (12): *I know it's weird and it's kind of embarrassing to admit, but I really like my stepmom. She is really nice and we were friends before she married my Dad. Everybody thinks you should hate your stepmother cuz stepmothers are evil, but mine isn't.*

****

Terri (34), a stay-at-home mom, and John (40), a pastor, of Boulder, Colorado had both been divorced for several years before meeting one another at church. Terri's daughter Amanda (5) and son Andrew (7) seemed to enjoy having a big brother, Jake (10) and a stepfather.

Amanda (5): *I like my new daddy. He's funny and he knows all the words to the SpongeBob song. He sings it in a funny voice that always makes me laugh.*

Jake (10): *Getting siblings was kind of cool, since I was an only child before. It was a good bonus I guess; except when they're brats.*

****

Cassidy (10) *I think the best way us kids have blended is when Dad and Sloane go out on Saturday nights. They have a date and go to dinner and stuff, and we stay home together. Last weekend after they left, all four of us went outside and played flashlight tag, and it was really fun! Kids should be allowed to just play together without the grown ups interfering.*

****

Family Pictures

Depending on the ages of the kids (say between three and 10), one helpful idea is to have the children draw a picture or a diagram of their blending family. Talk with them about everyone in the picture – their place in the family, their roles, who lives where and with whom, etc. This helps them visualize what new roles they may have, and as they discuss their pictures it helps them see the new family in a positive light. It is sometimes surprising to see how children view their families.

****

Monica: *We are very blessed in that we have virtually no problems with the kids beyond the typical "he poked me/she* looked at me" sibling-type stuff; mostly I think because of their ages. I really liked the idea of the family diagram so I asked Cameron if he would draw a picture of our family for me. He drew a very colorful and detailed picture of a house with two rooms. Each room had two stick figures in it. There were flowers, a tree and a cat (even though we don't have a cat), and a car in front of the house with another stick figure inside. I asked him to explain his picture to me and he said, "This is me and you cooking dinner," pointing to two figures, "and this is Lindy and Hailey" pointing to the other two figures.

I pointed to the car and asked, "Is this Steve?"

He said, "No, that's Daddy coming to take me to Chuck E. Cheese Pizza on Saturday!"

I didn't see Steve in the picture and I was afraid that he had been left out due to some hidden resentment toward him, so I asked Cameron, "But what about Steve, honey?"

And he said, "Oh, he's out back swimming in the pool."

****

Children can be very concrete thinkers. Try expanding the family picture to allow for grandparents, aunts and uncles, the stepparent's parents and siblings, and even cousins and step-cousins. This helps children see that they have many people in their lives that love them, and they can *visually* grasp how everyone is related.

****

Terri: *After two years of marriage we thought the children were adjusting well to stepfamily life. The only problem was Jake, who just couldn't seem to grasp the idea that my family was somehow connected to us and what that had to do with him. I have a sister, Barbara, but Jake hasn't met her* because she's a missionary and lives in Ghana. Every time Barbara's name came up in conversation, Jake would act all irritated and ask, "Who is she?"

I finally found several photos of my family of origin and of Barbara on the mission field, and showed them to Jake. I explained to him who everybody is in the photos and how they're related to me and my kids. I think that seeing pictures of me with Barbara and photos of her in Africa made her seem a little more real to him.

****

Fear Factors

Take notice of your children's fear or insecurities surrounding the changes that will occur when the stepfamily forms. Ask pointed questions and discuss their feelings. Children's fears about their new stepfamily can run the gamut from being afraid of losing some of their privacy to being sent away. Thanks to Walt Disney, some of our children's only models of stepparents are wicked-witch-types who plot to get rid of the children. Just before our wedding, Lysa told David she was afraid that when I became her stepmother I was going to send her to boarding school. Ok, I admit, there were moments when I was tempted, but only because I had no idea how to suddenly handle having four children in the house!

Unfortunately, one of the ways children handle fear is to lash out at whatever is making them uncomfortable. Six months after our wedding, David and I were swimming in our pool with his children. Suddenly Lysa grabbed onto her father, hissed at me like a cat and said, "Mine! He's mine! He doesn't love you, he loves me!"

I remember mumbling something about being sure that her daddy loved us both, when she glared at me and hissed, "Infiltrator!"

First of all, I was impressed that this little nine-year-old girl knew what the word meant and had used it correctly. I immediately decided not to take it personally. Lysa was lashing out at me because she was afraid of losing her daddy's affection. She was testing to see how strong our marriage was and just how far she could push me.

So I did not react. I simply ignored her comment. The last thing I wanted to do was compete for my husband's affections with his daughter. Getting into an argument with a nine-year-old over who loves whom is never wise.

Don't Call Me Butthead

One of the biggest issues for the children is what name to call their new stepparent. We have seen several stepparents insist that they be called mom or dad, but this usually doesn't turn out well. It doesn't matter if the biological parents were parted due to divorce or death; in the child's mind he or she already has a mom and a dad, and a stepparent will not fulfill that relationship. Insisting on being called mom or dad will only lead to anger and resentment.

A few children may come up with clever names for stepparents, like Poppy for a stepdad, but we have found that the majority of children choose to call their stepparent by their first name. When David and I first married, Lysa wanted to call me *Madrastra*, which is the Peruvian-Spanish word for stepmother. It's a mouthful and a bit formal, so she just calls me Susan. Chase has taken to calling me Susie. I told him that no one except my first grade teacher has ever called me Susie, and he is welcome to. It's cute and makes me feel like we have a special bond. At any rate, it should be the child's choice as to what to call the stepparent as long as they have an explicit understanding that derogatory or disrespectful names like Butthead are not allowed.

****

Brit (46), a retired Marine, and Melanie (36), a teacher, live in Atlanta, Georgia. Brit has two sons by his first marriage: Javon (22) and Jamal (21), both of whom are in the Air Force. Brit's second wife died shortly after the birth of their daughter, Jasmine (5). Melanie was previously married and has no biological children, but legally adopted Jasmine shortly after their wedding in 2003.

Melanie: *The thing that has surprised me about being a stepmother is how well everyone accepted me. There has never been one negative attitude or problem. Jasmine calls me Mommy. Of course, she was only 2 when we married. The boys were both pretty well grown – in their late teens – when we married. Javon was in boot camp and unable to come to the wedding, but Jamal was there. They have both been very supportive and loving. They both call me Miss Melanie. It's a southern thing.*
Britt: *Ironically, I was the one who had trouble with the whole stepfamily thing. Jasmine's mother died just a few days after giving birth to her, and so it was just me and Jasmine for two years. You know, Daddy's little girl. But after the wedding it was "Mommy this" and "Mommy that" and I'm thinking, what about Daddy? I felt really left out, like suddenly there was this "girls club" in my house and I wasn't invited. A friend of mine who has daughters told me to give it time; that Jasmine was only 3 and she was figuring out what it means to be a girl and bonding with Melanie, which was what I wanted. He said, "By the time she's 5, it'll be all about Daddy again." He was right.*

****

Focus On the Positive

As a stepparent, you will find that there will be days when it seems like nothing you do is right and the children wish you were dead. On those days, the only advice we have is to take a deep breath and remind yourself that it is not about you. On the other days, when things go well and the children are acting like they might even like you, savor those moments.

Focus on the little victories and write them down! Keep a journal of your stepfamily journey. For example, when you get a goodbye hug from your stepdaughter, jot that down. If your stepson asks you to come to his baseball game, note the date. Periodically look back and reread your journal entries. Last summer I tucked Lysa into bed one night, kissed her on the forehead and told her I love her. She actually said, "I love you too".

You may be surprised how far you've come as a family, in a relatively short time. However, keep in mind that blending is a process and it may seem like you take two steps backward for every one step forward – and God only knows how many steps sideways! Just keep moving.

Here We Go Again

Don't be surprised if you have to revisit some of these issues repeatedly. Just because your stepson accepted you when he was 5, doesn't mean he won't test the waters all over again when he's 7. Or 10. Or 13. Or every year in between. It may seem like a never-ending process, and in some ways it is. Remember, blending is not an event or a competition. The goal is for everyone in the family to become a team, and eventually to win together. In the following chapter we will take a look at ways to become a team, and not just a bunch of people wearing similar uniforms.

Advice from the Blender:

- It's not about you, so don't take it personally
- Love never happens in an instant – give it time to develop and grow
- Children will need to work through and talk about their feelings – talk with them
- Children may need a visual "who's who" of the family
- Let the children decide what to call their new stepparent
- Keep track of all the positive things that happen
- Just when you think things are fine, you may have to revisit certain issues and talk about them all over again - it's a never-ending process

Questions for Reflection and Discussion with the Entire Family

Let the kids know it's OK to be honest about their feelings and it's OK if they don't love everyone right away, but they should still be respectful to everyone in the family.

What do the kids *really* think about the new stepfamily arrangements?

Ask them: What are you afraid of? What are you worried about?

Has the relationship between kids and stepparent changed? How?

What is working, what is not working and how have you handled it?

Is there another blending family or a counselor that you can turn to when you need help?

What is the biggest obstacle for the kids? How are they dealing with it? How can you help the kids make the transition?

What will the kids call their new stepparent? Is this their choice or yours?

Focus on the positive: What is the **best** thing that has happened regarding the kids?

CHAPTER 5

Choosing your battles
Blending parenting skills

◎

"If it's not one thing, it's your mother."
~ Carol Caputo-Haeick

For me, one of the most surprising aspects of becoming a stepmother was that the love didn't just magically *flow* from my heart toward David's children. It's easy to love the children you gave birth to, even when they are annoying. It's *not* so easy with stepchildren. Sometimes it's downright difficult to love a little girl who refuses to get ready for bed or brush her teeth (or do anything else you ask her to do) because she's stubbornly repeating, "I want Daddy!"

Kids will be kids. They can be noisy, rude, irritating, clumsy, throwing food or a tantrum one minute; and the next minute they are sweet, smiling, lovable, helpful and climbing up on your lap for a hug. Of course, the sweet moments are what make parenting worthwhile, but when you are a stepparent, it may seem like those sweet moments hardly ever come. Hang in there – eventually they will.

No Triangles Allowed

Research shows that the single most destructive thing a husband or wife can do in a blended family is to side with their biological child against their spouse[20]. In counseling circles this is called "triangulation" and triangulation kills communication (think *strangulation*). Before you start thinking that this will never happen in your new family, understand that you are dealing with human beings who have been hurt. Hurting people tend to hurt other people, and your first reaction, your instinct will be to defend your progeny. During heated discussions, presenting a united front with your spouse at all times *will not feel natural*. However, uniting is imperative to the health of your marriage and your blending family.

If your child is disagreeing with your spouse or a stepsibling, resist the urge to jump to your child's defense. Encourage the two people involved in the dispute to talk it out with each other. If your child comes to you and complains, "He's being unfair to me!" Or, "She lets him do this, and won't let me …" simply tell your child to discuss it with the one they are having the problem with.

I admit that sounds easier than it is. It's like telling a mother bear to go back to the cave when she sees someone messing with her cub. However, keep in mind that your goal as a parent is to help your child to grow into a responsible, functioning adult. Often they must be trained to do this by reasonably stating their position, learning to listen to others, and discovering how to compromise. In essence, your children must be taught to fight their own battles.

We have all heard the horror stories from teachers about parents who blindly defend their child against any and all "unfairness" on the part of the school system, threatening to sue everyone who gets in their way. Don't let that occur in your home. Encouraging your children to talk with the other person will do more to teach them effective communication and negotiation techniques than anything you could do *for* them. In short, don't allow communication triangles.

Mirror, Mirror

One way to avoid triangulation is for the entire family to learn a communication skill called "Mirroring". This is a technique that is taught in counseling sessions. It is a way to communicate that not only encourages each party to talk about their feelings, but also ensures they are heard and understood. In the mirroring exercise, two people sit opposite one another. They take turns speaking about their feelings while the other person listens. The listener is not allowed to interrupt or argue. (They will get a chance to respond later.) After the speaker is finished, the listener reflects the message back to the speaker – like a mirror – and asks if they heard the message correctly. If they heard the message correctly, the listener asks if there is more. Once the first speaker has said everything he or she needs to say, and the listener has clarified it, they switch roles so that the second person can be heard. It looks something like this:

Jack: *When you don't come to my daughter's softball games, it makes me feel like you don't care about her or our family. I get really angry that I have to take her to games by myself.*

Jill: *What I'm hearing you say is that it makes you mad that I don't come to your daughter's softball games. It makes you think that I don't care about her or you. Did I get that right?*

Jack: *Yes, that's about right.*

Jill: *Is there more?*

Jack: *Well, yes. It's not just the softball games. You don't seem to want to do anything with my kids. I get the feeling* *that they are an annoyance to you, and that you don't want to be their stepmom.*

Jill: *What I hear you saying is I'm giving you the impression that I don't want to be a stepmother or a part of this family at all; that the kids aren't important to me. Is that correct?*

Jack: *Yes.*

Jill: *Is there more?*

Jack: *No, that about covers it.*

Jill: *OK. I think I understand you. I'm sorry that I gave you the impression that I was annoyed by the kids. Being a stepmom is still all new to me, and it never occurred to me that my going to the softball games was important to you. I do want to be a part of this family, and I do want to be a good stepmom. I will try to be more involved with the kids and their activities from now on, OK?*

You may be thinking, "Nobody talks like that!" Mirroring may feel and sound awkward at first, but it is a great way to address emotional conflicts without resorting to raised voices, or circular arguments. Like any skill worth developing, mirroring takes a certain amount of patience and practice, but it will greatly improve your family's ability to communicate effectively. Try it.

It's Not About You

Every honest stepparent will admit there are days when they are tempted to run screaming from the house, wanting to catch the next flight to Bora-Bora or Timbuktu. I confess that I have also indulged such fantasies, but only because I had no idea what I was doing as a stepmother or how I was supposed to manage having four children, two of whom didn't like me very much.

Advice From The Blender

****

Doreen, a realtor, and Bill, a surgeon, live in Phoenix, Arizona. They are in their 50s and have been married for 12 years. As a career woman with no children of her own, becoming a stepmother to Bill's three grown children was a challenge for Doreen, and to become an instant stepgrandmother was a real eye-opener!

Doreen: *If I had one piece of advice for people who are marrying into a family it would be to remember that it's not about you. No matter what the situation or who says what, it's never about you. When I married Bill, his kids were in their 20s, and one daughter was already married. They had their own ways of doing things, their own way of interacting with their father. None of that was going to change just because I was suddenly in the picture! So my advice is to get over yourself, get your ego out of the way and try to enjoy each moment as it comes.*

****

"Both researchers and clinical experts agree that the stepparent role is more difficult and less clearly defined than the parent role[21]." The keys to building a relationship with your stepchild are patience and *never* taking anything personally. For example:

- When your stepson won't eat what you cook, don't take it personally.
- When your stepdaughter pretends you don't exist, don't take it personally.
- When your stepchildren refuse to wear the clothes you buy them, don't take it personally.

Advice From The Blender

- When they loudly say to their mother, "That guy you married is ordering us around again" don't take it personally!
- When they call you names or ignore you completely, *never* take it personally.

"How am I supposed to not take it personally?" you ask. First of all, breathe. Second, keep in mind that it's not about you! The children are most likely *hurting inside*. They are either:

a) Comparing your actions to those of their biological parent.
b) Dealing with loyalty issues between you and their biological parent.
c) Testing to see how strong your marriage really is.
d) Trying to make sure that you are for real.
e) Angry, sad, or feeling a million other things all at once.
f) All of the above.

Nine times out of 10, the answer is "all of the above".

****

Sloane: *It has been an ... experience ... becoming a stepmom. I really love all of our kids, but I have to admit there are days when I don't like Jason's two very much. They won't do anything I suggest, they won't eat what I cook or wear the clothes I buy for them. I don't think they do it intentionally; it's just that they have this loyalty thing with their mom. Like they're betraying her if they enjoy something I provide. It is very frustrating!*

Jason: *I agree. They are very conflicted about their mother. For instance, since Sloane's studio is in our house* she's here when the kids get home from school. Cassidy actually said to her the other day, "Why are you always here? Why don't you get a real job?" I noticed it with Cole last week. Sloane bought a Veggie Tales movie for him, thinking he'd like to watch it with her, and he immediately said, "I don't like Veggie Tales. They're dumb." This was new – he's always liked Veggie Tales.

Sloane: (laughing) *Lucky for us, Jason does most of the cooking; otherwise his kids would starve over their unspoken rule of never eating anything I cook! I have figured out that it really has nothing to do with me – they are getting mixed messages from their mom and are conflicted about that. So I try to just let it go.*

****

Remember that no one, including your stepchild, does anything because of you. Most of their actions are motivated by their own internal turmoil. Once you understand that very little of what people do or say is because of you, then you are free to not take things to heart.

Scary Movies

In order to avoid conflict over differing rules in different houses, we choose to use one simple word: *"and"*. For example, I know that both of my children are sensitive to frightening images. We have all lost a lot of sleep over scary things that go bump in the night. When Zonie was 11 she came home from a weekend at her dad's and said that she wanted to watch *The Shining,* an R-rated horror movie which was on TV. She insisted, "Dad lets me watch horror movies!" I simply replied, "*And* in this house, we aren't allowed to watch them." That ended the discussion. After all, house rules are house rules.

Advice From The Blender

****

Sasha (17): *The confusing thing for me was even if the rules were the same at both houses, they were more exaggerated at one house. At Dad's, it's like the end of the world if you break a rule. He goes totally crazy. At Mom's house the rules are still serious, but she and my stepdad are more understanding, and you don't get grounded for life.*

****

Brooke (15): *In my Dad's house everything's like mind your manners and go to church and it's really strict. At my Mom's house it's a lot more relaxed and we may have to cook for ourselves, but its fun. On the other hand, my Mom moves a lot so that kind of sucks because when we see her it's always in a new apartment and we have to help her unpack.*

****

Alexa (15): *Sometimes I feel like I have a split personality. I do one thing at Dad's, another at Mom's. My rooms are completely different; I act differently depending on which house I'm at. When I told Mom I have a pink flowery room at my Dad's she was totally shocked, cuz at her house everything about me is kind of Goth. Even though their rules are mostly the same, I act different at each house.*

****

The issue comes down to accepting that there may be different rules and different parenting styles in different homes[22]. David and I have come to learn that there is nothing we can do about the rules or different discipline styles in our kids' other homes and it doesn't do anyone any good to get upset about it. Likewise, our kids have learned to accept that some of the rules are a little more stringent in our house than they are elsewhere, but some are a bit more lax.

For instance, when my son Tanner wanted me to shave his head into a Mohawk, and when Zonie wanted to dye her beautiful blonde hair jet black, David and I said that was fine. Someone once told me "You have to choose the hill you want to die on". There are some things we are willing to battle over, but self-expressive fashion is not one of them. We would rather have our children be a little daring with their hairstyles (which grow out) in junior high school, than end up bailing them out of jail when they are 18. Granted, I don't know if allowing them a little self-expression now will guarantee that they will grow up to be good, law-abiding citizens, but I am willing to try it.

The Decibel Level

Couples need to understand that with more children comes more noise, more clutter and more chaos. They will all increase exponentially. Consequently, so will your stress levels. Discuss your expectations for the kids *with* the kids. Keep in mind that God values your family[23] and He wants it to work. Plan ahead for worst-case scenarios! This can help alleviate a lot of stress. What kind of worst-case scenario planning are we talking about?

- **Kool-Aid House:** This isn't as scary as it sounds. Set up some basic house rules: how many friends are allowed over at one time? Is there a safe place to play *outside*? What is the limit on snacks and sodas? Who is supervising?
- **Volume Levels:** What exactly constitutes TOO loud for the TV, video games, and music? Which TV shows/games/CDs are absolutely off limits?

Who chooses the TV show, video game or music? How long is each person's turn? Kitchen timers come in handy for this problem.
- **Shared Space:** If bedrooms and bathrooms must be shared between siblings: what are the rules for borrowing clothing and "stuff," decorating, keeping things neat, cleaning, allowing privacy, closing/locking the doors, etc?
- **Chores:** Who does which chores around the house? (No, the answer isn't "Mom") Make up a chart to avoid the arguments of, "I cleaned it last time!" and "She *never* does the dishes!" Make it fair – even if actual time spent in the home isn't equal, everyone should be responsible for the chores assigned to them.
- **Clutter:** Encourage everyone to in the house to pick up after themselves or the clutter will take on a life of its own.

Even when you have planned ahead for some of these things, living in a stepfamily is stressful. It's like having new roommates, only these roommates come in all shapes, sizes and age-groups; and some of them may not want to be there. Understanding this is crucial for living life in the blender. Find ways to alleviate stress for yourself and your spouse. Some effective ways of managing stepcouple stress are: going for walks together, making time to talk to each other, taking turns dealing with the children, praying together, instituting "quiet time" for everyone in the house, occasionally hiring a baby-sitter and keeping those date nights on your schedule.

It's Not Fair!

If there is one phrase in the stepchild vernacular that should be abolished but has somehow been elevated to the

Advice From The Blender

status of a fine whine, it is, "It's not fair!" Every parent and stepparent we spoke with has a story about their kids using this phrase. For some reason, most kids in blended families still cling to the idea that life should be absolutely fair and equitable in every instance, and they are very resolute in pointing out any and all perceived unfairness.

****

Sheila: *If I hear "it's not fair" one more time, I'm going to scream. My oldest son, Derek, said to me the other day, "It's not fair that the Smith kids get to stay home with you, and get Happy Meals for lunch." I was like, the Smith kids? Um, excuse me, you're ALL my kids! I pointed out that Nicky and Jilli are too young to go to school. I also pointed out that when Derek and Kyle were little they stayed home with me and got McDonald's for lunch occasionally too. But did that satisfy him? No, because somehow the entire universe is against him, and it's not fair!*

****

Sloane: *My kids have been on us about bedtimes. Our girls share a room and our boys share a room, so we put everyone to bed at the same time every night. Well apparently that's not fair, because Jason's kids are younger, so according to my two, they should have to go to bed earlier. It doesn't occur to them that staggering four bedtimes would stretch the whole bedtime thing out for hours!*

****

Karen: *Why my daughter suddenly felt it wasn't fair for her to do chores at our house I don't know, but suddenly it's unfair that she has to wash dishes. Mandy told me that Ariel* *should do the dishes even though she's only at our house three days a week, because 'it isn't fair' that Mandy has to do them every evening. So am I supposed to leave all the dirty dishes in the sink for days at a time, waiting for Ariel to come over? I don't think so!*

****

We believe that this protest against unfairness is really a complaint against something deeper. Chances are the children are not *really* complaining about bedtimes, chores or McDonald's Happy Meals, but about the fact that their lives were uprooted and overturned by events over which they had no control; namely your divorce (or the death of their parent), and your remarriage.

Children like predictability. They thrive on certainty and routine. Their routine was disrupted by events precipitated by the adults in their world and this is frightening to children. Then when you remarried, their routine was disrupted yet again. Your children did not ask to be thrust into a stepfamily, and more than likely they are not thrilled about this new development. It was not part of their plan, and it makes them feel insecure and out of control. Complaining about small things – the perceived unfairness of the moment – gives children a sense of control, especially when their complaints result in changes.

If your children begin complaining about things being unfair, consider that they might be feeling they have no control over anything. This type of situation calls for wisdom on the part of parents in blended families. If you give in to the children's complaints, and attempt to make all things fair, you will reinforce their perception that they can control YOU. This will result in a never-ending battle. Instead, help your children understand that life is not governed by the concept of limited good[24], and life is not always fair.

Allowing children to control some aspects of their own lives can be very positive. It teaches self-assurance and encourages good decision-making skills. One way to do this is to allow them to make some of the decisions – with proper guidance, of course – that directly affect their lives. For example, our boys, Tanner and Chase, share a bedroom. When it came time to paint the walls we allowed the boys to choose their own colors. As a result they have a bedroom that is half grass-green and half pumpkin-orange. They are certainly not colors *I* would have chosen, but by allowing the boys to decide how to decorate their bedroom, we gave them a sense of control and a sense of belonging. They worked together to decide where to place the posters and pictures on the walls. The entire process gave them a sense of joint ownership of their room, and they've never complained about it being unfair. We did the same thing with the girls regarding their bedroom. It took them more than a year and a half to finish the decorating, and I can't even begin to describe what it looks like, but it's their room.

Sticks and Stones

My mother always told me, "If you don't have anything nice to say, don't say anything at all." More often than not this was whispered through clenched teeth while navigating through a crowded church fellowship hall, but the lesson stuck with me. And even though on the playground we sang, "sticks and stones can break your bones, but names can never hurt you," the truth is words can and do hurt.

One of the best pieces of advice we have received from fellow blending families is this: Be kind to one another. Only speak words that will build each other up, not tear each other down[25]. Your home should be a place of refuge and safety for those who live there. It is a sad commentary on families today that people are mean and vicious to their own family members. When conversing with your family, think to yourself: Is what I am about to say helpful? Is it necessary? Is it kind? Would I say these words to my pastor, a judge, or the president? If the answer to those questions is "No," then close your mouth. Rephrase your comments to be helpful and kind.

****

Bill: *While we don't face the daily challenges of a traditional blended family, as none of my children are under one roof with us, we continually seek God's grace and wisdom as we negotiate our relationships with the adult children and the emerging dynamic of grandchildren who are becoming their own little people. Our greater challenge is probably maintaining relationships with all of them and always trying to be supportive and kind. It helps to look for the positive in every situation.*

****

Melanie: *Our family motto has been: Be open. Be honest. Be real. Be kind and gracious. We always try to think the best of each other and we guard our minds from negative, false thoughts that may creep in. It isn't always easy but keep working on it. Choose to be gracious with your family.*

Britt: *You know, so many folks try to read each other's minds ... like, "she must be trying to manipulate me" or "he's hiding something" and they react badly, before they even know the truth! You've got to be honest in your family but don't allow anything to be negative – your thoughts or your words. These are the people you're supposed to love! Treat them that way!*

****

Both Tony (35) and Angela (33) were widowed prior to their marriage two years ago. Combined, they have five children living with them in a suburb of Boston: his 4-year-old twin boys, her 3-year-old twin girls, and their 6-month-old son. Tony works in construction, and Angela stays at home with the children.

Angela: *I grew up in a house with lots of criticism. My parents were very judgmental, and could never see the good in anything. My first husband used to tease everybody. It was his way of being funny, but lots of times his comments were hurtful. So Tony and I try really hard not to criticize or tease each other or the kids, and we try to only say loving things. It's been fun to see the kids internalize this, and the boys are quick to point out when someone at preschool isn't saying nice things.*

****

Karl: *I see no reason to be negative. The Bible says, "A gentle answer turns away wrath, but a harsh word stirs up anger*[26].*" It's common sense. Of course, common sense isn't very common these days.*

****

You Can't Pick Your Relatives

Once you get to the point where you are building relationships within your home, you will inevitably realize that there are also relationships that require maintenance outside of your home. Some of these are your in-laws, your parents, your siblings, their spouses and their children. But wait, there's more! What about your ex-spouses, *their* parents, siblings, spouses and children? A divorce may dissolve a marriage, but it does not dissolve families. In the next chapter we will examine how extended family relationships evolve through the blending process.

Advice from the Blender:

- Don't take anything personally
- Choose the hill you want to die on
- Work up a plan for *everything*
- Don't triangulate your relationships
- Learn to communicate effectively
- Look past the obvious to find the deeper meaning
- Speak words that build up relationships
- Think before you speak

Questions for Reflection and Discussion

How will you handle discipline?

How will you decide on rules, curfews, and behavior expectations? What are the consequences?

What level of rebellion do you expect the kids to dish out? Plan ahead for it!

What, if anything, have you fought or argued over as a couple or as a family?

How do you, your spouse and your children communicate?

How can you improve your communications skills?

How do you manage stress? What kind of "stress busters" can you put into practice?

CHAPTER 6

In-laws, Outlaws and Theories of Relativity
The 'ex-tended' family experience

"If you ever start feeling like you have the goofiest, craziest, most dysfunctional family in the world, all you have to do is go to a state fair. Because five minutes at the fair, you'll be going, 'you know, we're alright. We are dang near royalty'."
~ *Jeff Foxworthy*

When you are blending your family, you may find that there are branches on your new family tree that don't seem to have anything at all to do with you. There will be branches on the family tree you might not want to acknowledge. There will be branches on your tree that you thought had been cut off or pruned back but are somehow still around. These errant branches could be on your side or on your spouse's side; but there will be an odd side to your new family. Just accept it.

In a blending family, at least one of the adults has a former spouse. No matter how much you might wish that they would just disappear, you WILL have to deal with them. One of the primary issues stepcouples have to contend with are the roles, responsibilities and expectations about their former spouses. For example, my former husband lives in another state. He loves our children, but due to his financial situation only sees them in the summer and during holidays. We rarely talk with him, unless there is an urgent situation involving travel plans for the kids. David's former wife, on the other hand, lives three miles from us, calls David and their children every day and stops by our house several times a week. In her mind just because David is now married to someone else does not mean that they can't interact with one another, spend holidays together and still be one big happy family! The situations with our former spouses are opposite extremes, and if David and I hadn't discussed the situations prior to our marriage it could have been a major point of contention. Obviously every situation is different. Expectations about the former spouse's role and responsibilities, and the reality of the situation may turn out to be vastly different. It's best to be prepared ahead of time.

Forgiveness

Most Christian counselors will tell you that when dealing with former spouses, the place to start is with forgiveness. While that may sound wonderful, it is not easy. Initially after a divorce, your relationship with your ex-spouse may be adversarial, but remember; when Jesus said to "turn the other cheek" He didn't have it in mind for you to *moon* your former spouse. The Bible says we should pray for our enemies and those that persecute us[27]. I can honestly tell you that as a Christian, I wanted to be able to pray for my ex-husband, but there were days when I could do nothing more than say, "God, YOU deal with him." I think God understands this type of prayer. And as time passed and my hurt and anger faded, I stopped praying for him to get hit by a bus. It took a few years and a lot of soul-searching for me to get to the point where I now pray that God will bless my ex-husband and his new wife.

I am reminded that when Jesus was on the cross, he forgave the people who sold him out; he forgave the soldiers who were pounding nails through his flesh saying, "Forgive them, Father, for they don't know what they are doing." However, I also noticed that when Jesus emerged from the tomb on Easter Sunday, he did not take Judas or the Roman soldiers out for brunch. Forgiveness does not necessarily mean reconciliation. Just because you are learning to forgive your ex-spouse does not mean you have to become best friends, especially in cases that involved betrayal or abuse. A cordial, respectful or business-like relationship would be considered an admirable goal in most cases.

Stepparent Roles

If you are a stepparent and the newcomer in the family unit, your job is to love your spouse, love the children, and support them all as best you can. You must let your spouse and his/her ex-spouse handle situations that affect their children together. Do not interfere with their job as parents, even when they have a difficult or contentious relationship. It isn't your place to run interference, pass messages or serve as a buffer between them, as tempting as it may be. Refrain from intercepting phone calls, e-mails or information that they require as parents. Doing so is inappropriate and can get downright dangerous.

****

Sloane's former husband remarried one month after their divorce was final.

Sloane: *My ex-husband's new wife immediately inserted herself into our lives insisting that all communication go through her, saying it would be easier. I admit, my ex and I didn't always communicate well, so at first I was relieved. It was easier to talk to her – she didn't yell at me. But after a while, I realized that he wasn't getting any of my messages and she was controlling everything about our relationship with our kids. Our only communication was through e-mail because she wanted a written record, and she would hang up the phone if I called their house.*

However, her e-mails became increasingly hostile and mean. She said I was manipulative and conniving. She accused me of lying to my ex-husband, neglecting my children and manipulating their expenses for my own financial gain. Every time I got an e-mail from her I ended up in tears! I finally confronted my ex-husband and it turns out he wasn't aware that any of this was going on! In fact, he'd been wondering why I never called him to talk about the kids. We have managed to find a way to speak to one another without his wife's interference, but there was a lot of damage done. I wouldn't trust her as far as I could throw her, and I have a really hard time letting my kids go visit them knowing what I do about her. However, I try to take the high road and be civil – even if it's through gritted teeth.

****

Ideally, a respectful and cordial relationship can be developed between former spouses and the new spouse. This takes a certain amount of work and a crash course in extreme diplomacy, but if everyone remembers that the goal is what is best for your children, it can be done.

Advice From The Blender

****

Doreen: *Interestingly, the least of our challenges is the relationship we have with both of Bill's ex-wives. We see Sara (wife #1) and her husband Glen at various family gatherings and these encounters are always pleasant. Nancy (wife #2) lives out of state, but due to some overlaps with our time-share schedule we have occasion to be in contact with her too. When I was recently recovering from major surgery I received a very kind get-well card from Sara and Glen, who are fellow believers. I know this is a stunning example of being joined with them in the Body of Christ, despite the history of divorce.*

****

Sometimes the single parent is left with an emotional void in their life after their former spouse has remarried and begun the blending process. This may emerge as a delayed reaction with jealousy, manipulation of the visitation schedule or hostility. Chances are, the underlying issue has more to do with the self-esteem of the parent who has not moved on, but it can be very difficult on the family that is trying to blend.

****

Elise (42), a human resources manager, and Scott (45), a mechanic, live in rural Montana on a ranch. They have been married nine years and have a son, Trey (6). It is Elise's first marriage, Scott's second. He has two daughters by his first marriage: Lark (18) and Katy (15).

Elise: *We don't see Scott's girls at all anymore and I know he misses them a lot. Their mother, who lives about 45 minutes away, usually makes them call and cancel their* visits saying she can't drive them out to the ranch, and they always have an excuse why we can't go see them. This has gone on almost every weekend for the past six years – basically since Trey was born. Before that, we saw the girls every weekend and had a great relationship with their mother! I'm sure that our having a baby had something to do with it. So now our life has settled into a routine between Trey, our jobs and the ranch – we have 22 horses, 50 some-odd cattle, a small herd of sheep and an assortment of cats - but I can tell that Scott would much rather have his girls here. Now that Lark is 18 we're hoping that she'll come visit of her own accord. It's just sad that they no longer have a relationship with their dad, or with their little brother.

****

Steve: *Monica's ex-husband is a pretty decent guy. We're on the same softball team at church, he's a great dad to Cameron and he always sends his child support on time. I've got no complaints there. On the other hand, my ex-wife, who was perfectly fine with our custody arrangements before Monica and I got married, keeps suing me for custody changes. We've been through five court hearings just this year trying to sort out the custody schedule because after a few months of it being one way, she changes her mind and wants something different. At the moment, Lindy and Hailey spend one week at my house and one week at hers, and that's been tough on them. I keep saying my ex-wife needs to find a hobby other than taking me to court.*

****

Advice From The Blender

Keeping Up With the Outlaws

While divorce dissolves marriages, it does not dissolve families. Children are still related to their grandparents, aunts, uncles and cousins from both sides of their family. Try to maintain contact with those relations – if not for yourself at least for the children. We have done this for our children. I still consider my first mother-in-law a good friend; I call her, exchange birthday and Christmas cards with her and send her pictures of Zonie and Tanner. She is always thrilled to hear about their activities or speak to them on the phone. Since David's former wife lives nearby with her mother, we do spend most holidays with them and we stay in contact with Lysa and Chase's other out-of-state relatives on their mom's side of the family.

When a remarriage occurs, "sides" of the family are added exponentially, increasing the amount of family members, and creating new relationships. For example, Lysa and Chase now have five grandparents: David's parents, their Mom's mother, and my parents. They also have great-grandmothers who are still living: one their Mom's side and one on mine. This concept may make sense on paper, but it is often difficult to relate to within your own family.

****

Angela: *I think that since the kids were all so young when Tony and I married, and because as twins they all sort of have each other, we really haven't had a problem blending as a family. They were all excited about having the new baby and getting to be big sisters and brothers. The problem is with Tony's parents. We get along fine – they like me – but for some reason they just can't accept my girls as their grandchildren.*

Tony: *At first we thought they were just taking their time getting used to the idea, but this past Christmas the boys got twice as many presents from my folks as the girls did. My mom even refers to the boys as her real grandchildren. I tried to explain that since Angie and I are married, the girls are real grandchildren too – it's not like they aren't real kids or that they're going to just go away. In fact, I'm adopting them. We're hoping that this'll kind of blow over before the kids get old enough to notice, but I'm not holding my breath. My parents are pretty set in their ways – and they just don't get it.*

****

It may not only be the extended family members who have trouble with this concept, so don't beat yourself up if you fall into this category. When my ex-husband married his new wife, my children were excited to tell me that they now had two new sets of grandparents and two new aunts (the new wife's mother and her husband, her father and his wife, and her younger sisters). I admit that I could not accept this. I had no idea who these people were – in my mind, they weren't at all related to my children. I resented all these strangers giving gifts to my kids at Christmas. After all, I had never met them.

A year later when I married David, his parents became grandparents to my children and his sister became their aunt. Suddenly I realized (much to my chagrin) that the relationships on their father's side of the family were no different – and it wasn't about me! (duh…) It simply means that my children have a "leafier family tree".

****

Advice From The Blender

Jennifer: *When Barry and I married, my kids were thrilled to get grandparents that lived in the same city! My first husband's family lived in Russia, so Alexa and Sasha only knew them from photos, and my parents live in California, so we only see them occasionally. Barry's parents and his brothers have been so wonderful about incorporating us into their family; including us in all their cultural traditions and loving us as if we'd always belonged.*

****

Marjorie: *Our families had always been close friends. We knew all each other's children and their children, and they all knew each other. Now we're all part of one family! It was lovely to become an "official" grandmother and great-grandmother to Karl's grandchildren. I always say the more the merrier!*

****

Culture Shock

When you blend your families, the worldview – the social and ethnic cultures – of both you and your spouse are incorporated into your new family culture. Your worldview has to do with your family of origin, your expectations and how you subconsciously "see" the world. However, in a more subtle way, the worldviews of your ex-spouses and their families will also play a prominent role in your blending family culture, especially for your children. Your children are influenced, both overtly and subconsciously, by the traditions, ethnic culture and social views of both of their parents. These influences are incorporated into their own worldview and that will not change just because their parents divorce.

Those parental ethnic/social/cultural influences will become a part of the worldview of the now-blending family.

****

Kelly: *I was aware of the ethnic differences between Randy and his first wife obviously, but I had no clue how deeply it affects relationships. I am learning what "family" means to the Hispanic community – that once you're family, you're always family. His ex-wife's relatives kept inviting Randy to their family gatherings, and I thought it was because they were in denial about their divorce. When they invited me too, I realized that they include him because in their eyes he's still family and now by extension so am I! My own family wasn't like that. Unless you were a blood relative, forget it. It's really nice to feel accepted and included.*

****

Karen: *Even though we all live in Texas, there are definitely cultural differences between Texans. Jon's ex-wife Sandi, is ... how do I put this politely ... from redneck stock. Her mother was married like six times, and apparently they moved around a lot. At the moment Sandi lives in a travel trailer at the edge of town and she waits tables at a cowboy bar. Not that there's anything inherently wrong with that, but she has this defensive attitude. Since both Jon and I have college educations, she thinks we're snobs. She's always telling Ariel not to worry about her grades; that education is over-rated, and that money isn't everything. OK, money isn't everything, but why set your sights so low? Why not encourage your kid to set goals? It's like she didn't succeed in life, so she can't stand it if anyone else does! Ariel loves her mother and defends her, which means we are always in conflict trying to counteract her attitude.*

Advice From The Blender

****

By being aware of the worldview phenomenon and learning to appreciate (or at least accept) the culture of your children's families, you will lessen the chance of misunderstandings and avoid unnecessary conflicts between members of your "ex-tended" family.

To Blend or Not to Blend

They say that nothing tests our character better than tangled Christmas lights and holiday dinners with your ex-spouse. OK, I made up that last part. However, the true test of how your family is blending will occur during holidays, so it is best to be prepared. In the following chapter, we'll examine how to keep Christ in Christmas when everything else in your home is in chaos, and how to handle other worst-case scenarios.

Advice from the Blender:

- Family is not a four-letter word
- Remember to focus on what is best for the kids
- Pray for your ex-tended family members
- Forgive, move on and take the high road
- Delve into a cultural study of your family
- Learn extreme diplomacy!

Advice From The Blender

Questions for Reflection and Discussion

How will you manage relationships with "the other parents" – the former spouses? What about the other parents' parents ("the outlaws")?

What is your visitation/custody/support situation and how is it working?

Have you begun to forgive your former spouse(s)? How about yourself?

How will you manage the in-laws, outlaws, grandparents - new and old - cousins, etc.?

How extended is your family now?

What can you do both personally, and as a family, to develop and maintain good relationships with your extended family?

What cultural variations are influencing your blending family worldview?

What steps can you take to focus on what is best for the children?

CHAPTER 7

Holidays and Other Worst-case Scenarios
What blending *really* means

⊚

"Some people live and learn, and some people just live."

~ *Sharon King*

Holidays will test your blending family's strength like nothing else. Whether they are birthdays, Christmas, Valentine's Day or even the Fourth of July, holidays overwhelm us with expectation, pleasure, disappointment, ritual and tradition. They reveal our most fundamental emotions. Think back to when you were a child. Do you have a perfect holiday memory? How about a terrible holiday memory? Now hold those thoughts for one second and recognize that *no one* in your blending family shares those memories with you. The members of your family each have their own memories and their own ideas of what holidays mean, and chances are they are nothing like yours. For blending families, holidays can be particularly stressful, not just because they evoke strong emotions, expectations and memories, but because it will become painfully clear that family members do *not* all share the same expectations, traditions and rituals.

Christmas is traditionally a time of nostalgia, cherished memories and family customs. Whether the tradition is baking gingerbread people from great-grandma's recipe, going to Christmas Eve service at midnight, visiting Santa at the mall, cutting down your own Christmas tree or singing carols at the homeless shelter downtown, every family has certain traditions that they keep during the holiday season. The reason we carry on traditions is because they preserve our emotional connections with our families of origin, our heritage and our childhoods.

Christmas in a blended family can become a time of frustration and resentment if the traditions from one side of the family get tossed by the wayside in favor of traditions from the other side. Very rarely does anyone do this intentionally, but unless the family members discuss their expectations about Christmas and come to an agreement about which family traditions to incorporate into the blended family, wounded feelings and conflict are inevitable.

****

Amber (12): *I always loved Christmas, but after Daddy and Kelly got married I hated it. First thing they did was buy a gigantic, fake tree that had lights on it already. Then Kelly bought tons of ornaments and most of them were like, blue. I thought it looked tacky. Brooke helped them decorate the tree, but I didn't. I miss having a real tree that smells good and has familiar ornaments.*

****

Advice From The Blender

Angela: *Our first Christmas together as a family was just horrible. I had always spent Christmas with my family, and Tony had always spent it with his, so we thought we would just make the rounds and see both families on Christmas day. We woke up at 6:00 on Christmas morning, opened presents with the kids, ate breakfast, got everybody dressed and into the car, then drove an hour north to see my parents who live in New Hampshire. We opened presents, ate a second breakfast, jumped back in the car and drove another hour west to see Tony's brother and his family who live near the Vermont line. We opened presents, ate lunch, piled back in the car and drove 45 minutes to my sister's house in Massachusetts to visit with her family. We opened presents, ate lunch again, then got in the car and drove back toward Boston to visit Tony's parents. We opened more presents, forced ourselves to eat dinner, and drove home at a little after midnight – all with four whiney toddlers. It was absolutely THE worst Christmas we've ever had. We vowed never to travel on a holiday again. If anybody wants to see us they come to our house!*

****

Steve: *Our first Christmas together as a family was tough, mainly because we weren't actually together. My ex-wife insisted I come spend Christmas morning at her house so the girls could open their stockings with both of their parents there. I was torn ... I wanted to see my girls, but I also wanted to spend Christmas with Monica and Cameron. So, this year Monica and I decided that our family would celebrate Christmas on Christmas Eve. We told the kids that Santa comes a day early to the homes of blended families. It was actually a lot less stressful. We opened gifts, had a wonderful dinner, went to church together – no pressure. I spent Christmas morning with the girls at their mom's, Monica* *went to see her parents, and Cameron spent Christmas day with his dad. It's not ideal, but what is?*

****

The words "but we've *always* done it this way" can be polarizing – try not to go there when discussing the holidays. Be prepared to encounter resistance and issues you never anticipated, such as who will put up the Christmas lights (or if you have lights at all) and whether you plan to decorate your Christmas tree the day after Thanksgiving or the day before Christmas Eve. Be open to new or different ideas when it comes to the holiday decorating, or try to incorporate several ideas from everyone. Get the kids involved if you can, but don't force the issue. If one of them chooses not to participate, that's OK – leave them alone.

Brainstorm together ways to start a *new* holiday tradition – one that only your blended family holds. For instance, when David and I married, we decided to purchase a new Christmas ornament for each family member every year. I try to purchase ornaments (or things that can double as ornaments) while we are on our family vacations in order to preserve those memories. A few years ago I bought each of us an individual Lego minifigure key chain, and last year we all acquired a small cruise-related ornament. Someday when our children move into their own homes they can take their own box of ornaments with them to decorate their Christmas trees.

The Reason for the Season

The key to keeping the peace at Christmas time is to remember exactly what the holiday is about – the birth of our Savior. When you consider what is truly important during the season, remember that Jesus' family did not have a Christmas tree, nor did they sing "Grandma Got Run Over By A Reindeer". Christmas is really about God loving humanity so much that He sent Jesus into our world as the ultimate gift to us[28]. Jesus was born an infant in order to live and grow as a human being, fully comprehending and empathizing with every trial and obstacle we humans face, from birth to death[29]. Jesus lived His life as an example to us[30], showing us that there is so much more to life than human beings usually settle for. He died on the cross as payment for our sins, voluntarily taking on the penalty that we deserved. He rose from the dead[31] and returned to heaven, and anybody who believes in Him gets to live with Him forever[32]. That is what Christmas is really all about – the most important gift ever given, the gift of love and eternal life from God to us. Remind yourself and your family *why* you celebrate Christmas, and the particulars of *how* you celebrate may not seem so important.

One Disaster after Another

Every stepfamily is unique and made up of individuals who are also unique. There are many challenges that stepfamilies have to deal with, and what constitutes the normal course of events for one family might be regarded as an unmitigated disaster for another family. Most of the stepfamilies we interviewed had a "worst-case scenario" to tell us about. Some were holiday-centered and others were not. However, when we consider what blending a family really means, these worst-case situations ultimately supply the definitive ingredients for successful blending – compromise, boundaries, compassion and patience.

****

Karen: *Life was hard enough with the 'yours, mine and ours' kids, but when we added two more teenagers into the* mix, our life just became insane. We've got kids in four separate schools, three sports leagues, two dance teams, not to mention four different churches! I had always had this image of our family going to church together every Sunday, but that just hasn't happened for us. Jon was raised Catholic, and I was raised Methodist. We compromised by going to the Presbyterian Church together and we had Dylan baptized there. Mandy goes to the Southern Baptist church with her dad, because they have a great youth group. Ariel's mom recently began attending the Church of Christ, so Ariel wanted to go with her. The older boys have always gone to the Pentecostal Church, and didn't want to change churches, and we don't blame them.

Jon: It's a little crazy around here on Sundays with everyone going in different directions, but I figure it's all Christianity, right? At least they're all still going to church.

****

Sloane: I suppose our worst-case scenario was our child support situation. As an artist, I don't make a huge amount of money on a regular basis. We were doing OK on Jason's income but honestly, we relied on child support from Alisha and Thatcher's dad to make ends meet. About a year after Jason and I got married, that suddenly stopped. My ex-husband – who was never the most stable guy in the world – suddenly quit his job and moved to another state. Six months later, he did it again. At the beginning of last year, the child support enforcement people finally caught up to him. We received one $200 payment, then he was "laid off", or so he claimed. He moved again, and has gone through two more jobs this year. It's absolutely infuriating that he can't keep a job or be responsible for his own children. Needless to say, we've learned to be self-reliant, but I think the hardest thing for me is maintaining my composure about this in front of my kids. This isn't an issue for them to deal with and I try not to criticize their father in front of them, even when I want to scream.

****

John: *Terri and I are both born-again Christians and live out our faith in our everyday life. We believe that God brought us together, and it is our desire to honor Him in our marriage and family life. We met each other at my church (I'm the pastor). After we were introduced, I was totally smitten. She was a beautiful, very busy single mother of two children, working full time to make ends meet. She and I began to talk more and more at church on Sundays. After a few months, we finally spent a day together at the junior high youth group pool party – we were the official chaperones. I realized that everything about being with Terri felt right. We talked about marriage that very first day, and it seemed totally natural. I never really proposed – we just knew we would get married.*

We ended up waiting a full year to marry because that was how long our premarital counseling sessions took. As a pastor, I am held to a higher standard than most and our church elder board wanted to make sure we were all on the same page regarding divorce and remarriage, theologically. I had been married to Jake's mom – a woman with many problems – for seven years. She left me, Jake, and the church for another woman. Terri had been married to an unbeliever with a drug addiction. He walked out just before Amanda was born. We established that there was no hope for reconciliation with either of our former spouses, but we had to work through all of those concerns with our elder board through prayer, counseling and Bible study. That was very difficult and the waiting was very difficult – for all of us. But in the end we knew God brought our family together. We keep Him at the center of our marriage and our family and pray together every day.

My advice to couples contemplating remarriage would be to make sure you are equally yoked. It is so important that you are both believers. Do things God's way not your own way. And don't try to go it alone. Get with other believers who will support you in your marriage and blending your family.

****

When David and I married, one of our goals for our children was that they be able to spend time with our extended family that live close by – David's parents, his former wife and her family. As a result, we have spent most of our holidays with them which has forced all of us to put aside our differences and focus on the bigger picture: what is best for our children. Last Easter will always stand out for us as the definitive example of a blended family gathering. The guests included: David, myself and our four kids; his parents, my parents and two of our single friends; David's former wife, her sister and her husband and their two kids; her brother and his partner; her mother, and her uncle and grandmother from Peru, who do not speak any English. The children had fun hunting for eggs together, as the adults joined together to cook an enormous dinner while trying to communicate in two languages. It was a day of smiles, laughter and yes, even genuine love as we celebrated the resurrection of our Savior together.

Several people we know are astounded that we are able to spend our holidays with David's former wife in this manner. However, we are quick to point out that our common faith transcends obstacles like age, language, culture, lifestyle, church affiliation and divorce. As Christians, we are all part of the same family.

Are We There Yet?

Now that we have unpacked our bags, begun to be deliberate about choosing to love our family, and survived the holidays, where do we go from here? In the following chapter we will consider what the entire blending process entails and outline a comprehensive family blending recipe that you can put into practice in your own family.

Advice from the Blender:

- Learn to compromise
- Let the little things go
- Set boundaries
- Don't go it alone
- Remember *why* you celebrate holidays

Questions for Reflection and Discussion

With whom and where will the kids spend holidays, and how flexible is this schedule?

What do you foresee as the biggest challenge for your particular family?

What are you willing to compromise on, and what is non-negotiable?

What boundaries do you need to put in place?

What is the worst-case scenario you can imagine and has it materialized?

How will you manage this situation, should it arise? Do you have a Plan B?

How can you extend compassion and patience toward your family during the holidays?

Do you have support, and/or someone you can team up with for encouragement as a blending family?

CHAPTER 8

The House Blend
Your family blending recipe

⊚

*"Let me s'plain... no, there is too much.
Let me sum up."*
~ Inigo Montoya in The Princess Bride

When David and I first began to blend our families I read a few articles and books about stepfamilies, curious as to what we were in for. I was dismayed by what I read: almost 70% of remarriages with children end in divorce[33], most remarriages do not last five years, it can take up to 10 years for a stepfamily to blend[34], and if you have children between the ages of 10 and 16 you are condemning them to a life of psychological pain and failed relationships once you remarry. I kept thinking, this can't be right – there is absolutely no hope here! There has to be something else; something between *The Brady Bunch* and these doomsday predictions. There is. Blending a family can be done and it can be fun. You will need a little advice, some back up, a lot of determination and a good recipe, but you can succeed.

Ingredient #1: Realistic Expectations

In chapter one, we examined the differences between nuclear and blended families and some of the expectations you and your family may have about the blending process. The first ingredient in your House Blend recipe is realistic expectations. These can be acquired by analyzing what you are expecting, wishing and hoping, and tossing out the unrealistic expectations in favor of a more realistic approach.

The best way to make sure your expectations are realistic is to sit down and talk about what you envision for your family in the following areas:

- Finances
- Plans and dreams for the future
- Ex-spouses
- Family and friends
- Work and leisure time
- Household roles and division of chores
- Sex and time alone
- Religion and spirituality

This not a complete list, of course, but it was designed to give you several ideas from which to begin your discussion of expectations. Add your own topics as they come to mind. Discuss how your expectations may differ from those of your spouse and your children. Write down everything that you agree on, as well as topics you may not agree on but can consider compromising on. This will give you a written recipe to follow and refer to in case conflict arises in one of these areas. Remember that blending is a process not an event, and it takes time.

Ingredient #2: A Strong Marriage

In chapter two we looked at the types of emotional and psychological baggage you have collected over the years, both as an individual and as a family, as well as how to unpack it. The critical point here is that in order to be a healthy functioning family, each individual member must be a healthy functioning person. Get to know yourself, and become the best person you can be. Get to know your spouse. Get to know your children. Be empathetic and understanding about their baggage. Realize that some bags are easier to unpack than others, and some may require professional counseling.

Some of the baggage issues that you will need to address are:

- Spiritual issues
- Divorce or death matters
- Skeletons in the family closet
- Work and career
- Emotional traumas
- Finances
- Conflict management skills
- Sexuality

Once you have begun to unpack your baggage and gotten to know each other as people, you can focus on the process of blending and on prioritizing your marriage. As a couple, sit down together and discuss your wants and needs in the following areas, and rank them in order of priority:

- Spirituality
- Recreation and hobbies
- Time: me, us, family
- Intellectual pursuits
- Music, the arts, sports

- Work and career
- Parenting styles
- Household roles: housework, cooking, etc.
- Love languages
- Emotional closeness and communication
- Conflict management
- Sex

Again, this list is by no means complete, but is designed to give you a starting point for discussion about what you want in your marriage. Be completely honest with one another, write down and work out any differences you may have regarding these areas. For instance, if the husband ranks sex as his number one need in the marriage and the wife ranks emotional closeness and communication as her number one need, try to coordinate the two so that both people get their needs met. Consider that it doesn't have to be one or the other – look for win-win solutions. Be determined about making your marriage successful. A strong marriage is a key ingredient to a thriving blended family.

Ingredient #3: A United Parenting Team

In chapter three we explored some of the package deal dynamics and roadblocks you may encounter when you are blending your family. While the assumption may be that the children will accept the new family arrangement and that everyone will come together seamlessly, the truth is you can not just add water and stir to create an instant family. Kids are part of the package and they have feelings too – some of which aren't pretty. It takes a lot of hard work to blend a family.

Emotional bonding requires a concerted effort on the part of everyone in a blending family, although the majority of that effort will fall on the adults. As parents you must make the effort to psychologically and emotionally commit to the entire family, schedule time to build the family connections, support the children's activities, and find creative ways for everyone to get to know one another.

Some bonding suggestions include:

- Eat family dinners together as often as possible.
- Use a color-coded calendar system.
- Support each child's extracurricular activities.
- Commit to taking a family vacation every year.
- If a weeklong vacation is not possible, be deliberate about taking mini-vacations.
- Start a Friday night tradition of pizza and movies.
- Get to know your stepchildren.
- Spend time with all of the children one-on-one.

The adults in the household set the tone for the family. If the parental tone is disjointed or adversarial (i.e.: my kids vs. your kids; us vs. them) the kids will sense the disconnect, twist it and use to their advantage. However, if the parents think like a team, are supportive of each other and the family, and have a sense of humor, the children will be more likely to feel secure and loved and will be more accepting of the new family dynamics. The key to bonding as a blended family is to *choose* to love your new family members. You got a package deal – marry one, get one (or more) free! Make the decision and the effort to love them all. A strong parenting team is essential to a healthy blending family.

Ingredient #4: TLC – Time, Love, Consistency

In chapter four we discussed the way children typically respond when their family moves into the blender. When parents remarry, kids are forced to face the reality of mom and dad never reconciling, sort out changing birth orders, manage conflicting emotions about new family members, and somehow cope with events in their lives over which they have no control. To make matters worse, they are often expected to accept all of these changes without complaint. It can be a very confusing, frustrating and uncertain time in the child's life, and when children are confused, frustrated or uncertain, they tend to act out.

The crucial ingredient needed to take care of the children in your House Blend is TLC: Time, Love and Consistency. Understand that the children's emotions are overwhelming, and in order to process these things, they need time. Lots of time. Do not expect instant love and acceptance on the part of your stepchildren.

Remember that children often deal with strong emotions in bits and pieces. The child may pretend that nothing has changed, and act as if living in a blending family doesn't bother them at all. Or they may act out sporadically with alternating periods of anger, sadness and happiness. All of these strong emotions may manifest themselves in behavioral problems which *seem* to have no rational connection to any precipitating event.

As a parent or stepparent, you will be in a much better position to facilitate the changes going on in your children's lives by responding to them with love, compassion, patience and understanding. This means being conscious of the fact that your stepchildren are dealing with many changes in their lives, and reacting in anger will only exacerbate the situation. It means taking a step back and trying to analyze why your normally sweet daughter is suddenly belligerent, or why your boisterous stepson has become quiet and withdrawn. It means asking a lot of questions and saying a lot of prayers. And it means revisiting certain issues over and over again.

Practice consistency. Be consistent in your expectations of all your family members, and how you live together in your shared space. Plan ahead and write things down. Be consistent about loving your new family members, even when they do not reciprocate – *especially* when they do not reciprocate.

Keep in mind that blending is a process and it may seem like you take two steps backward for every one step forward – and God only knows how many steps sideways! Don't give up. Just keep moving.

Ingredient #5: Exceptional Communication Skills

In chapter five we analyzed the importance of learning to communicate effectively as a family. Excellent communication skills are important in all families, but are essential in blending families. Given that at least two distinct communication styles will be brought together when you blend your family, it is imperative that every member of the family learns to avoid triangulation and learns to communicate clearly.

Triangulation means deliberately intervening in a conflict or dispute that has nothing to do with you. It could mean siding with your biological child against your spouse. For example, when your spouse is disciplining your child, it may be instinctual to jump to your child's defense. However, doing so is not a healthy way to teach your child about respect, discipline or effective communication.

Take the time to learn several communication skills, such as the mirroring technique. Mirroring is a way to communicate that not only encourages each party to talk about their feelings, but also ensures they are heard and understood. Mirroring may feel awkward at first, but it is a great way to address emotional conflicts without resorting to raised voices or circular arguments. Like any skill worth developing, mirroring takes a certain amount of patience and practice, but it will greatly improve your family's ability to communicate effectively.

Advice From The Blender

Living in a stepfamily is stressful. It's like having several new roommates; roommates that come in all shapes, sizes and age-groups; and some of them may not want to be there. It will be stressful. Understanding this is crucial for living life in the blender. Find ways to alleviate stress for yourself and your spouse.

Some effective ways of managing stepcouple stress are:

- Go for walks together.
- Make time to talk every day.
- Take turns dealing with the children.
- Pray together.
- Institute a "quiet time" for everyone in the house.
- Keep those date nights on your calendar.

Above all, speak kindly to one another and don't take anything personally. Keep in mind that no one, including your stepchild, does anything because of you. Most of their actions are motivated by their own internal thoughts or conflicts. You will be free to let things go and not take them personally, once you understand that very little of what people do or say is because of you.

Ingredient #6: A Common Goal: What's Best for the Children

In chapter six we took a look at what it means to belong to an "ex-tended" family. While divorce dissolves marriages, it does not dissolve families. There can be many sides to a family; families are infinitely expandable. Therefore, do not expect anyone from the "ex" side of your family to vanish. You will eventually have to interact with them, and it is best to learn to do so with forgiveness, grace and courtesy. One way to begin this process is to pray for your ex-spouse and your extended family.

Ideally, a respectful and cordial relationship can be developed between the former spouses and the new spouse. This takes a certain amount of conscious effort and skillful diplomacy, but if everyone remembers that the common goal is what is best for the children, it can be done. Set aside your differences for the sake of the kids. Having a common goal is a crucial ingredient in your House Blend recipe.

Part of that goal is to understand that the worldviews of your ex-spouses and their families will play a role in your blending family culture, especially for your children. Children are influenced, both overtly and subconsciously, by the traditions, ethnic culture and social views of both of their parents. These influences are incorporated into their own worldview and that will not change just because their parents divorce. Those parental ethnic/social/cultural influences will become a part of the worldview of the now-blending family. By being aware of the worldview phenomenon and learning to be respectful of the culture of your children's families, you will lessen the chance of misunderstandings and avoid unnecessary conflicts between members of your extended family. Remember: always take the high road and focus on what is best for the children.

Ingredient #7: Flexibility

In chapter seven we examined how holidays can affect your blending family and how to best manage them. Holidays can overwhelm us with expectation, pleasure, ritual and tradition. They reveal our most fundamental emotions. For blending families holidays can be particularly stressful, not just because they evoke strong emotions, expectations and memories, but because it will become painfully clear that family members do *not* all share the same expectations, traditions and rituals.

The best way to cope with the holidays is to be flexible and learn to compromise. I am reminded that during storms, some trees are dislodged and some are not. When strong winds blow the trees that survive are the ones which can bend. They are strong, yet flexible. This is a great analogy for a blending family to take to heart. One of the most important ingredients for your House Blend is flexibility.

Remind yourself and your family *why* you celebrate holidays, and the particulars of *how* you celebrate may not seem so important. Learn not to worry about the details, and adopt new ideas and traditions as a family. Find another blending family to compare notes with and ask for help when you need it.

As time passes, you will inevitably encounter a "worst-case scenario" as a blending family. Whether it is a family acceptance issue, a financial setback, a rebellious child, or simply learning to let go of the "happily ever after" fantasy, prepare yourself and work out a contingency plan. This goes back to having realistic expectations for you and your family.

Ingredient #8: Prayer

As you engage in this process of blending your family, there will be moments when it seems like nothing is working. You will add all the right ingredients in the correct order, push the "Blend" button and…your children will refuse to get along with their stepsiblings, your spouse will retreat to the den, your ex-spouse will become increasingly hostile, and you will wonder what the heck you were thinking trying to blend a family!

Several months ago I felt the same way. I was almost finished writing this book; the publisher was on board, the cover was designed, the editing process was almost complete. At the same time Lysa was making snarky remarks about my lack of culinary skills, Tanner and Chase were arguing over whose turn it was to play the X-Box, David was nowhere to be found, Zonie was complaining that Lysa messed up their room *again*, and I'm thinking to myself, "Why am I writing this book? I'm failing at everything I've written! How can I give advice to blending families when I can't even get my own family to blend?"

So I carefully added the final ingredient to our House Blend: prayer. It is amazing how quickly doubt can creep into our hearts and minds and how quickly we can be made to feel completely inadequate. However, it is equally amazing how fast God answers our prayers. A friend of mine reminded me that everything in my life leading up to this moment is meant to be used for God's purpose. If our family experiences a few bumps in the blender it is because we need to be reminded that blending is a process. These bumps remind us that if David and I were perfect parents in a perfect family, we would have no need for God. These bumps remind us that we are far from perfect.

So pray[35]. Talk with God. Ask Him to help you through those days when you doubt yourself, your spouse, your kids and your family's ability to blend. Ask Him to lift you up when you feel inadequate. Ask Him to smooth out the bumps. Talk to God because He cares for you and your family[36]. He wants you to succeed as a family – a family who just happens to be living in a blender.

Advice From the Blender:

Your House Blend Recipe

Gently blend all ingredients:

- Realistic Expectations
- A Strong Marriage
- A United Parenting Team
- TLC – Time, Love, Consistency
- Exceptional Communication Skills
- A Common Goal: What's Best for the Children
- Flexibility
- Prayer

Allow the House Blend to infuse over time. Serve with unconditional love.

Appendix A

Resource List

The following books are ones we have read, used and found to be relevant, and a few that were recommended by the families we interviewed. Books are listed alphabetically by author and the list is not complete or exhaustive. Also included are Personality Inventories and where to purchase them.

Marriage:

Chapman, Gary, (1995). *The Five Love Languages: How to express heartfelt commitment to your mate.* Chicago, Illinois: Northfield Publishing.

> Gary has also written books on the love languages of children and teens, as well as books about healthy families.

Gottman, John M. (1995). *Why Marriages Succeed or Fail.* New York: Simon & Schuster.

> This is the classic book on marriage and communication.

Gottman, John M. (2000). *The Seven Principles for Making Marriage Work.* New York: Three Rivers Press.

Gudgel, David R. (2003) *Before You Live Together.* Ventura, California: Regal Books.

Harley, Willard F. Jr., (1986, 2001). *His Needs, Her Needs: Building an Affair-Proof Marriage.* Grand Rapids, Michigan: Revell.

> This book is invaluable – we recommend it to every newlywed couple we know.

Johnson, Greg and Yorkey, Mike, (1994). *The Second Decade of Love.* Wheaton, Illinois: Tyndale House Publishers.

> This book is geared more towards first marriages, but it has great information for couples with children who want to keep the romance alive. I'm not sure if this book is still in print, but you can still find it on Amazon.com.

Smalley, Gary and Trent, John, (1992, 2006) *The Two Sides of Love.* Wheaton, Illinois: Tyndale House Publishers.

> This book has an entire section on personality types and how they interact with one another. Gary's books and resources can be found on his Web site: www.dnaofrelationships.com. John's books and resource material can be found on his Web site: www.strongfamilies.org.

Blending families:

Advice from the Blender Online.

> This website features Blender Q&A, free articles, advice from kids and adults, and a monthly newsletter. www.advicefromtheblender.com.

Adkins, Kay, (2004). *I'm Not Your Kid: A Christians Guide to a Healthy Stepfamily.* Grand Rapids, MI: Baker Books.

> Kay has good insight into how children react to blending family dynamics.

Becnel, Moe and Paige, (2000). *God Breaths On Blended Families: A Testimony of the Becnel Family.* Baton Rouge, Louisiana: Healing Place Productions, Inc.

> The Becnels also have a Web site: www.blendingafamily.com.

Deal, Ron. *The Smart Stepfamily: Seven Steps to a Healthy Family.* Minneapolis, Minnesota: Bethany House Publishers (2002).

> More of Ron's resources: free articles, Q&A, books and a blog are available on his Web site: www.successfulstepfamilies.com.

Gillespie, Natalie Nichols, (2004). *The Stepfamily Survival Guide.* Grand Rapids, Michigan: Revell.

Natalie is a stepmom with seven kids and writes from the heart. The book contains a painful reminder that fighting over the children through the court system may be more costly than you think.

Hetherington, E. M. and Kelly, J. (2002). *For Better or For Worse: Divorce Reconsidered.* New York: W.W. Norton & Co.

This book reads like a psychological study on divorce but it contains lots of interesting information on how divorce affects children. Valuable if you are interested in what makes people tick.

Kolbaba, Ginger, (2006). *Surprised by Remarriage: A Guide to the Happily-Even-After.* Grand Rapids, Michigan: Revell.

Parrott, Les and Leslie. (2001). *Saving Your Second Marriage Before It Starts.* Grand Rapids, Michigan: Zondervan.

Parziale, Jeff and Judi (2002). *Looking Before You Leap ... Again! Preparing Yourself for the Adventures and Challenges of Remarriage.* Tucson, Arizona: InStep Ministries.

Jeff and Judi also have a 10-session group study available called *Second Chances: Preparing for Remarriage in the 21st Century.*
Find their books and resources online at: www.instepministries.com.

Parenting:

Kimmell, Tim (2005). *Grace-Based Parenting*. Nashville, Tennessee: The W Publishing Group.

> Tim is the expert on Christian parenting. This book is powerful and I highly recommend it. Tim's other parenting books and resources can be found on his Web site: www.family-matters.net.

Omartian, Stormie (1995). *The Power of a Praying Parent*. Eugene, Oregon: Harvest House Publishers.

Otto, Donna (1997). *The Stay at Home Mom*. Eugene, Oregon: Harvest House Publishers.

Otto, Donna and Buchanan, Anne Christian (2004). *Finding Your Purpose As A Mom: How to Build Your Home on Holy Ground*. Eugene, Oregon: Harvest House Publishers.

Smalley, Gary and Trent, John, (2004) *The Blessing*. Nashville, Tennessee: Thomas Nelson Books.

> This little book is a classic and was recently reissued. I recommend this for all parents who want to learn how to love their kids and stepkids unconditionally.

Finances:

Burkett, Larry (2001). *Family Financial Workbook*. Chicago, Illinois: Moody Press.

Larry has written countless books on managing money, and they're all good.

Orman, Suze, (2000). *9 Steps to Financial Freedom.* New York: Three Rivers Press.

Suze has built an empire teaching people how to manage their money by discovering the psychology of money and what it means to them. This book is not Christian, but has some valuable information just the same.

Ramsey, Dave (2003). *Financial Peace Revisited.* New York: Viking.

Dave is the Christian guru of finances. Even if you think you know everything about your money, read this book anyway.

Surviving/healing abuse:

Tracy, Steve (2005). *Mending the Soul: Understanding and healing abuse.* Grand Rapids, Michigan: Zondervan.

Wilson, Sandra D. (2002). *Released from Shame, revised edition.* Downers Grove, Illinois: Intervarsity Press.

Wilson, Sandra D. (2001). *Hurt People Hurt People: Hope and Healing for Yourself & Your Relationships.* Grand Rapids, Michigan: Discovery House Publishers.

Personality Inventories

The Couples Checkup

Married Couples – Falling in love is the easy part. Learning to get along during the ups and downs of marriage can be much more difficult. The Married Couples Checkup is a practical, personal resource designed to enhance and strengthen your marriage.

Premarital Couples – You're ready to get married, but how healthy is your relationship with your spouse-to-be? The Premarital Couples Checkup will help you start your relationship off on the right foot by facilitating open, honest communication.

The Couples Checkup will be automatically customized to match your life and relationship stage. You and your partner will be guided through a series of thought-provoking questions. Your answers – on a variety of topics – are then immediately processed to produce an extensive report designed to help you identify your relationship strengths and areas that need improvement. The cost for The Couples Checkup, full report and discussion guide is $29.95.

Available at: www.successfulstepfamilies.com.

Marriage Insights

Build oneness and increase understanding in your marriage! The Marriage Insights Assessment is an eye-opening, in-depth assessment that helps couples grow in their understanding and appreciation of each other. The online process delivers a comprehensive report full of personal insight and application for you and your spouse. Get ready for a valuable marriage experience!

You will receive a 24-page report on your individual and relationship strengths and keys to motivating your spouse according to his or her strengths. Included are communication insights that increase oneness, keys to effective communication and decreasing conflict, as well as a visual picture of how you compliment your spouse's God-given strengths that can lead to an opportunity to affirm your mate's special qualities. Assessments are also available for families. The cost for the assessment and report is $26.95.

Available at: www.leadingfromyourstrengths.com.

Appendix B

Bible Verses for Blending Families

Children

Psalms 127:3 – Behold, children are a gift of the Lord.

Psalms 22:6 – Train up a child in the way he or she should go, even when they are old they will not depart from it.

Deuteronomy 6:5-7 – You shall love the Lord your God with all your heart and with all your soul and with all your might. These words, which I am commanding you today, shall be on your heart. You shall teach them diligently to your [children] and shall talk of them when you sit in your house and when you walk by the way and when you lie down and when you rise up.

Psalms 23:13 – Do not hold back discipline from the child.

Ephesians 6:1-4 – Children, obey your parents in the Lord, for this is right. Honor your father and mother (which is the first commandment with a promise), so that it may be well with you, and that you may live long on the earth. Fathers, do not provoke your children to anger, but bring them up in the discipline and instruction of the Lord.

Relationships in the Family

Ruth 1:16 – Where you go, I will go, and where you lodge, I will lodge. Your people shall be my people, and your God, my God.

Proverbs 17:17 – A friend loves at all times.

Ephesians 4:1-2 – Walk in a manner worthy of the calling with which you have been called, with all humility and gentleness, with patience, showing tolerance for one another in love.

Philippians 2:1-5 – Therefore if there is any encouragement in Christ, if there is any consolation of love, if there is any fellowship of the Spirit, if any affection and compassion, make my joy complete by being of the same mind, maintaining the same love, united in spirit, intent on one purpose. Do nothing from selfishness or empty conceit, but with humility of mind regard one another as more important than yourselves; do not merely look out for your own personal interests, but also for the interests of others. Have this attitude in yourselves which was also in Christ Jesus.

Galatians 5:21-23, 25-26 – But the fruit of the Spirit is love, joy, peace, patience, kindness, goodness, faithfulness, gentleness, self-control; against such things there is no law. If we live by the Spirit, let us also walk by the Spirit. Let us not become boastful, challenging one another, [or] envying one another.

Ephesians 4:32 – Be kind to one another, tender-hearted, forgiving each other, just as God in Christ has forgiven you.

Colossians 3:18-21 18 – Wives, be respectful to your husbands, as is fitting in the Lord. Husbands love your wives and do not be embittered against them. Children, be obedient to your parents in all things, for this is well-pleasing to the Lord. Fathers, do not exasperate your children, so that they will not lose heart.

Marriage

Genesis 2:18 – Then the Lord God said, "It is not good for the man to be alone; I will make him a helper [strong companion] suitable [completing, corresponding to] for him." (Amplified)

Hebrews 13:4 – Marriage is to be held in honor among all, and the marriage bed is to be undefiled.

Mark 10:6-9 – But from the beginning of creation, God made them male and female. For this reason a man shall leave his father and mother, and the two shall become one flesh; so they are no longer two, but one flesh. What therefore God has joined together let no one separate.

1 Peter 3:1-4, 7-9 – In the same way, you wives, be submissive to your own husbands so that even if any of them are disobedient to the word, they may be won without a word by the behavior of their wives, as they observe your chaste and respectful behavior. Your adornment must not be merely external – braiding the hair, and wearing gold jewelry, or putting on dresses; but let it be the hidden person of the heart, with the imperishable quality of a gentle and quiet spirit, which is precious in the sight of God.

You husbands in the same way, live with your wives in an understanding way, as with someone weaker, since she is a woman; and show her honor as a fellow heir of the grace of life, so that your prayers will not be hindered. To sum up, all of you be harmonious, sympathetic, brotherly, kindhearted, and humble in spirit; not returning evil for evil or insult for insult, but giving a blessing instead.

1 Corinthians 11:11 – However, in the Lord, neither is woman independent of man, nor is man independent of woman.

Love

Proverbs 22:11 – He who loves purity of heart and whose speech is gracious, the king is his friend.

1 Corinthians 13:4-8 – Love is patient, love is kind and is not jealous; love does not brag and is not arrogant, does not act unbecomingly; it does not seek its own, is not provoked, does not take into account a wrong suffered, does not rejoice in unrighteousness, but rejoices with the truth; [Love] bears all things, believes all things, hopes all things, endures all things. Love never fails.

John 13:34 – "A new commandment I give to you, that you love one another, even as I have loved you, that you also love one another."

Ephesians 5:25-31,33 – Husbands, love your wives, just as Christ also loved the church and gave Himself up for her, … So husbands ought also to love their own wives as their own bodies. He who loves his own wife loves himself; for no one ever hated his own flesh, but nourishes and cherishes it, just as Christ also does the church, because we are members of His body. For this reason a man shall leave his father and mother and shall be joined to his wife, and the two shall become one flesh… each individual among you also is to love his own wife even as himself, and the wife must see to it that she respects her husband.

1 John 4:18-21 – There is no fear in love; but perfect love casts out fear, because fear involves punishment, and the one who fears is not perfected in love. We love, because He first loved us. If someone says, "I love God," and hates his brother, he is a liar; for the one who does not love his brother whom he has seen, cannot love God whom he has not seen. And this commandment we have from Him, that the one who loves God should love his brother also.

Romans 13:8-10 – Owe nothing to anyone except to love one another; for he who loves his neighbor has fulfilled the law. For this, "You shall not commit adultery, you shall not murder, you shall not steal, you shall not covet," and if there is any other commandment, it is summed up in this saying, "You shall love your neighbor as yourself." Love does no wrong to a neighbor; therefore love is the fulfillment of the law.

1 Peter 4:8-9 – Above all, keep fervent in your love for one another, because love covers a multitude of sins. Be hospitable to one another without complaint.

1 Corinthians 16:14 – Let all that you do be done in love.

Relationships with Ex-spouses and Ex-tended family

Matthew 5:44-48 – "But I say to you, love your enemies and pray for those who persecute you, so that you may be sons of your Father who is in heaven; for He causes His sun to rise on the evil and the good, and sends rain on the righteous and the unrighteous. For if you love those who love you, what reward do you have? Do not even the tax collectors do the same? If you greet only your brothers, what more are you doing than others? Do not even the Gentiles do the same? Therefore you are to be perfect, as your heavenly Father is perfect.

Ephesians 4:31 – Let all bitterness and wrath and anger and clamor and slander be put away from you, along with all malice.

1 Timothy 5:8 – But if anyone does not provide for his own, and especially for those of his household, he has denied the faith and is worse than an unbeliever.

Stress

Proverbs 3: 5-6 – Trust in the Lord with all your heart, and do not lean on your own understanding. In all your ways acknowledge Him; And He will make your paths straight.

Advice From The Blender

1 Peter 5:7 – Cast all your anxiety on Him because He cares for you.

John 14:1 – Do not let your heart be troubled.

John 16:33 – These things I have spoken to you, so that in Me you may have peace. In the world you will have tribulation, but take courage; I have overcome the world.

Notes

1. Hetherington, Dr. E. Mavis, and John Kelly, *For Better or For Worse: Divorce Reconsidered*. New York, NY: W.W. Norton and Co., Inc. 2002. Ron Deal, author and president of Successful Stepfamilies, quotes these statistics in an article on remarriage and rising divorce rates. The article can be accessed on the Internet at www.successfulstepfamilies.com.

2. Deal, Ron, "Stepfamilies: Who are they & how are they different?" Building a Successful Stepfamily Seminar. AMFM Conference, Scottsdale Arizona. July 2006.

3. Becnel, Moe and Paige, *God Breathes on Blended Families*. See Resource List in Appendix A.

4. Parziale, Drs. Jeff and Judi, "Second Chances." See Resource list.

5. Custis James, Carolyn, "A New Beginning?" Whitby Forum Newsletter, January 2007. Available at: http://www.whitbyforum.com/common/content.asp?PAGE=239&CONTENT=768

6. Chapman, Gary, *The Five Love Languages.* See Resource List.

7. Genesis 2:18, 24 "Then the Lord God said, 'It is not good for the man to be alone, I will make a helper suitable for him.'...For this reason a man shall leave his father and his mother and be joined to his wife; and they shall become one flesh." Matthew 19:4-6 "And He answered and said, 'Have you not read that He who created them from the beginning made them male and female' and said, 'For this reason a man shall leave his father and mother and be joined to his wife and the two shall become one flesh'? So they are no longer two, but one flesh. What therefore God has joined together let no man separate."

8. Luke 3:23 "Now Jesus himself was about thirty years old when he began his ministry. He was the son, *so it was thought,* of Joseph..." (italics added). What a great statement about a stepparent. No one knew that Joseph was the stepfather of Jesus – everyone thought Jesus was Joseph's son. Joseph took on the responsibilities that the angel gave him to name Jesus and to raise him (Matthew 1:19-24). Naming a child was the responsibility of a father in Jewish custom. Joseph is found in every other reference with Mary and Jesus – at Jesus' birth and dedication, when Jesus is lost in Jerusalem, and so on. We do not hear Joseph mentioned after Jesus began his ministry and most scholars think that he had passed away by that time. Paige and Moe Becnel note that "Joseph left an awesome legacy. Note that his legacy was based on his relationship with Jesus, not with his natural sons or daughters. We as stepparents need to step up and embrace all of the children that God has brought into

our world to influence, treating them and doing for them as though they were our own".

9. Personality Inventories can be purchased online from Insights International, and SuccessfulStepfamilies.com – see Appendix A for ordering information.

10. Ron Deal, *The Smart Stepfamily,* Minneapolis, Minnesota: Bethany House, 2002, page 94.

11. John 1:8-9: "If we say that we have no sin, we are deceiving ourselves and the truth is not in us. But if we confess our sins, He is faithful and righteous to forgive us our sins and to cleanse us from all unrighteousness."

12. John Gottman, *Why Marriages Succeed or Fail.* New York: Simon & Schuster 1995. pages 166-168.

13. Hetherington, ibid. page 167.

14. Jim Killam, "Dangerous Crossing." *Marriage Partnership Magazine,* Spring 2004. page 48.

15. See Appendix B for Bible verses pertaining to marriage.

16. Lyn Rhoden, "Stepfamilies in Therapy." Article available at: www.saafamilies.org.

17. Wheeler, Tom, "They Ganged Up On Me." 2003, Changing Families Ministries, Mt. Pleasant, South Carolina. www.changingfamilies.com.

18. Everett Worthington, *Counseling Before Marriage,* Dallas, Texas: Word, Incorporated, 1990. page 94.

19. Rhoden, ibid.

20. Killam, ibid. page 48.

21. Kay Pasley, et al., "What We Know About The Role Of The Stepparent," www.saafamilies.org/education/articles/research/pasley-2-93.htm

22. Deal, Ron, *The Smart Stepfamily.* page 134.

23. Psalms 127:1, 3: "Unless the Lord builds the house, they labor in vain who build it...Behold, children are a gift of the Lord."

24. The concept of limited good is similar to that of love being a pie, described in chapter 4. It is the belief is that if something good happens to person A, then that same good cannot happen to person B. In essence, person A stole the "goodness" from person B. In a variation of this view, if person A has something good, then person B will automatically get something bad instead. The concept of limited good is widely held in non-western societies.

25. Ephesians 4:29,32: "Let no unwholesome word proceed from your mouth, but only such a word as is good for edification according to the need of the moment, so that it will give grace to those who hear ... Be kind to one another, tender-hearted, forgiving each other, just as God in Christ also has forgiven you.

26. Proverbs 15:1: "A gentle answer turns away wrath, but a harsh word stirs up anger".

Advice From The Blender

27. Matthew 5:44: "But I say to you, love your enemies and pray for those who persecute you."

28. John 3:16-17: "For God so loved the world that He gave His only begotten Son, that whoever believes in Him shall not perish but have eternal life. For God did not send the Son into the world to judge the world, but that the world might be saved through Him".

29. Matthew 1:18-25: "Now the birth of Jesus Christ was as follows: when His mother Mary had been betrothed to Joseph, before they came together she was found to be with child by the Holy Spirit. And Joseph her husband, being a righteous man and not wanting to disgrace her, planned to send her away secretly. But when he had considered this, behold, an angel of the Lord appeared to him in a dream, saying, "Joseph, son of David, do not be afraid to take Mary as your wife; for the Child who has been conceived in her is of the Holy Spirit. She will bear a Son; and you shall call His name Jesus, for He will save His people from their sins." Now all this took place to fulfill what was spoken by the Lord through the prophet: "Behold, the virgin shall be with child and shall bear a Son, and they shall call His name Immanuel," which translated means, "God with us." And Joseph awoke from his sleep and did as the angel of the Lord commanded him, and took Mary as his wife, but kept her a virgin until she gave birth to a Son; and he called His name Jesus".

Hebrews 4:15: "For we do not have a high priest who cannot sympathize with our weaknesses, but One who has been tempted in all things as we are, yet without sin."

30. John 18:37: "For this I have been born, and for this I have come into the world, to testify to the truth."

31. Luke 24:1-12: "But on the first day of the week, at early dawn, they came to the tomb bringing the spices which they had prepared. And they found the stone rolled away from the tomb, but when they entered, they did not find the body of the Lord Jesus. While they were perplexed about this, behold, two men suddenly stood near them in dazzling clothing; and as the women were terrified and bowed their faces to the ground, the men said to them, "Why do you seek the living One among the dead? He is not here, but He has risen. Remember how He spoke to you while He was still in Galilee, saying that the Son of Man must be delivered into the hands of sinful men, and be crucified, and the third day rise again." And they remembered His words, and returned from the tomb and reported all these things to the eleven and to all the rest. Now they were Mary Magdalene and Joanna and Mary the mother of James; also the other women with them were telling these things to the apostles. But these words appeared to them as nonsense, and they would not believe them. But Peter got up and ran to the tomb; stooping and looking in, he saw the linen wrappings only; and he went away to his home, marveling at what had happened."

1 Corinthians 15:3-4: "For I delivered to you as of first importance what I also received, that Christ died for our sins according to the Scriptures, and that He was buried, and that He was raised on the third day according to the Scriptures".

32. John 11:25: "Jesus said to her, 'I am the resurrection and the life; whoever believes in Me will live even if he dies."

33. Statistics available at: http://www.stepfamilies.info/faqs/factsheet.php

34. Deal, Ron. *The Smart Stepfamily,* page 40

35. Mark 11:24: "Therefore I say to you, all things for which you pray and ask, believe that you have received them, and they will be granted to you."

Philippians 4:6: "Be anxious for nothing, but in everything by prayer and supplication with thanksgiving let your requests be made known to God."

Isaiah 65:24: "It will also come to pass that before they call, I will answer; and while they are still speaking, I will hear."

36. 1 Peter 5:7: "Cast all your anxiety on Him because He cares for you."

Printed in the United States
122176LV00002B/79/A